In this coloring book, titled "Cosmic Awakening: Celestial Mandalas," I invite you to embark on a journey of exploration and contemplation of the wonders of the cosmos through creative expression.

By coloring these mandalas, you not only fill in the blanks with vibrant pigments, but you also bring to life your own inner journey of self-discovery and cosmic connection.

May this book be a refuge for the weary mind, a sanctuary for the restless soul, and a beacon of inspiration for the explorers of the cosmos that reside within each of us.

May these Celestial Mandalas guide you on a journey of cosmic awakening, where art and the cosmos unite in an eternal dance of light and color.

So, grab your colored pencils, let your imagination soar and begin your coloring journey to the farthest reaches of the universe.

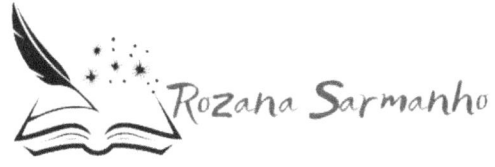

Rozana Sarmanho

This Book Belongs to:

○———————————————————————————————○

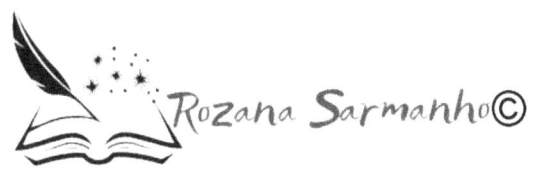

Test Color Page

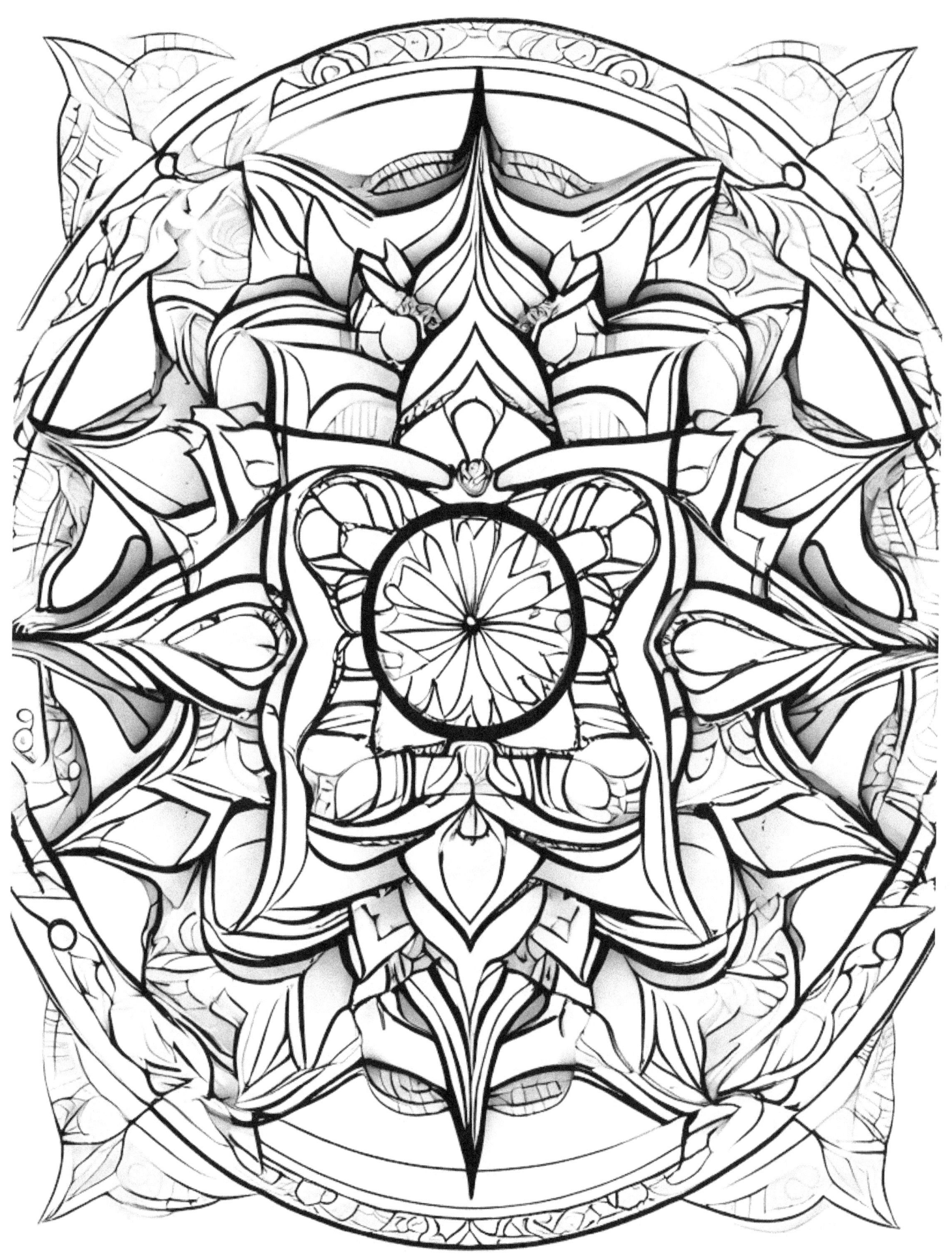

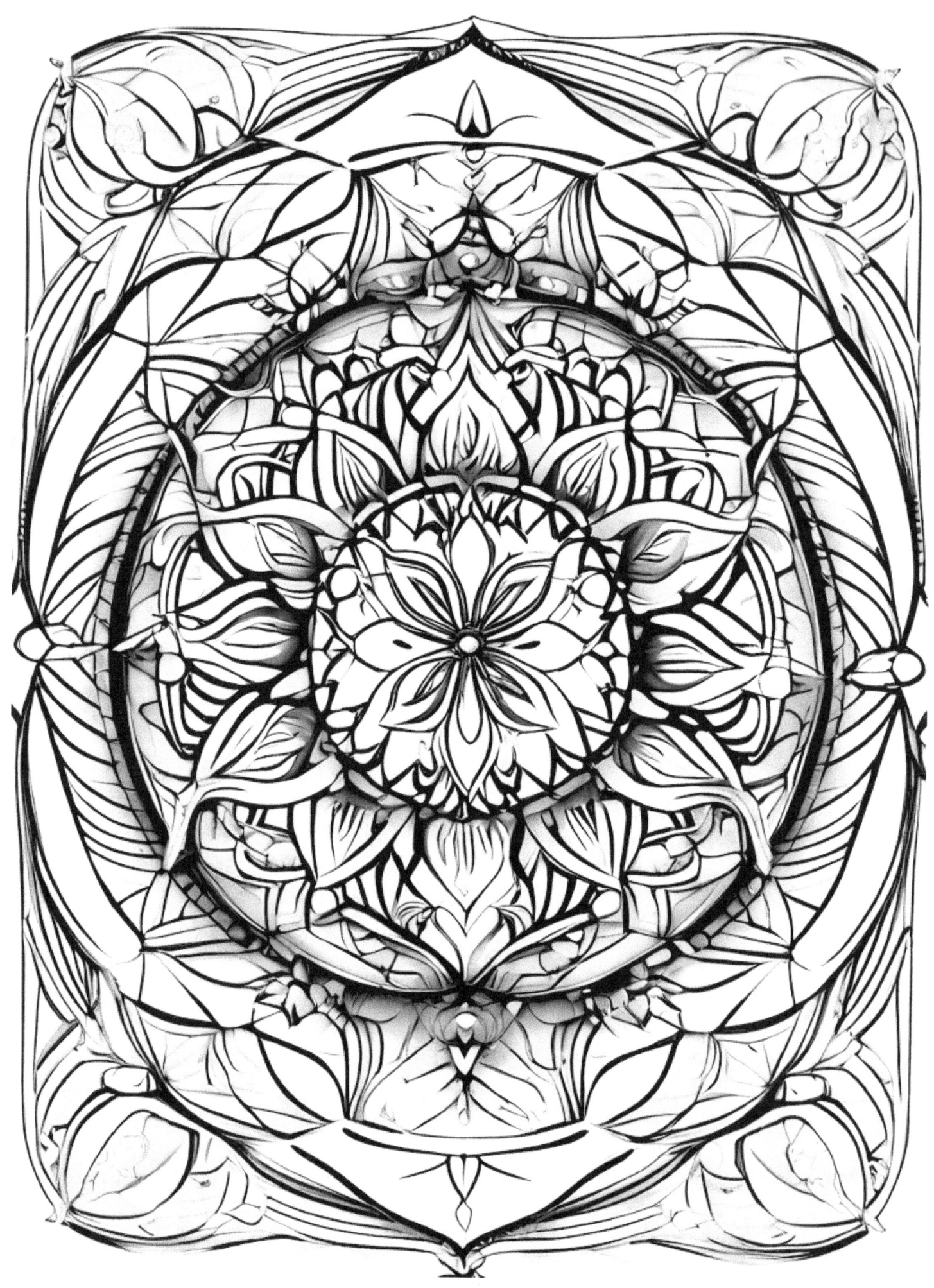

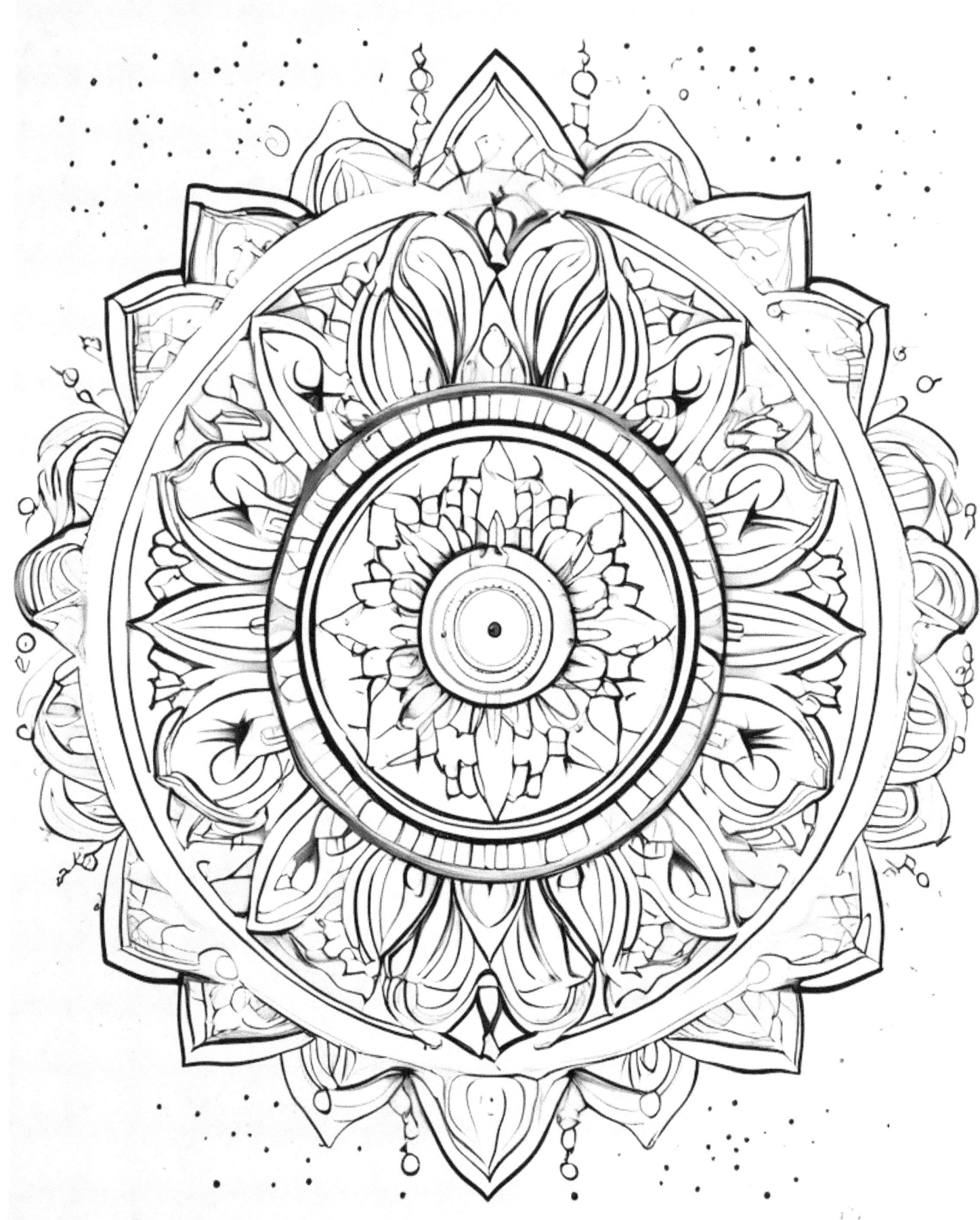

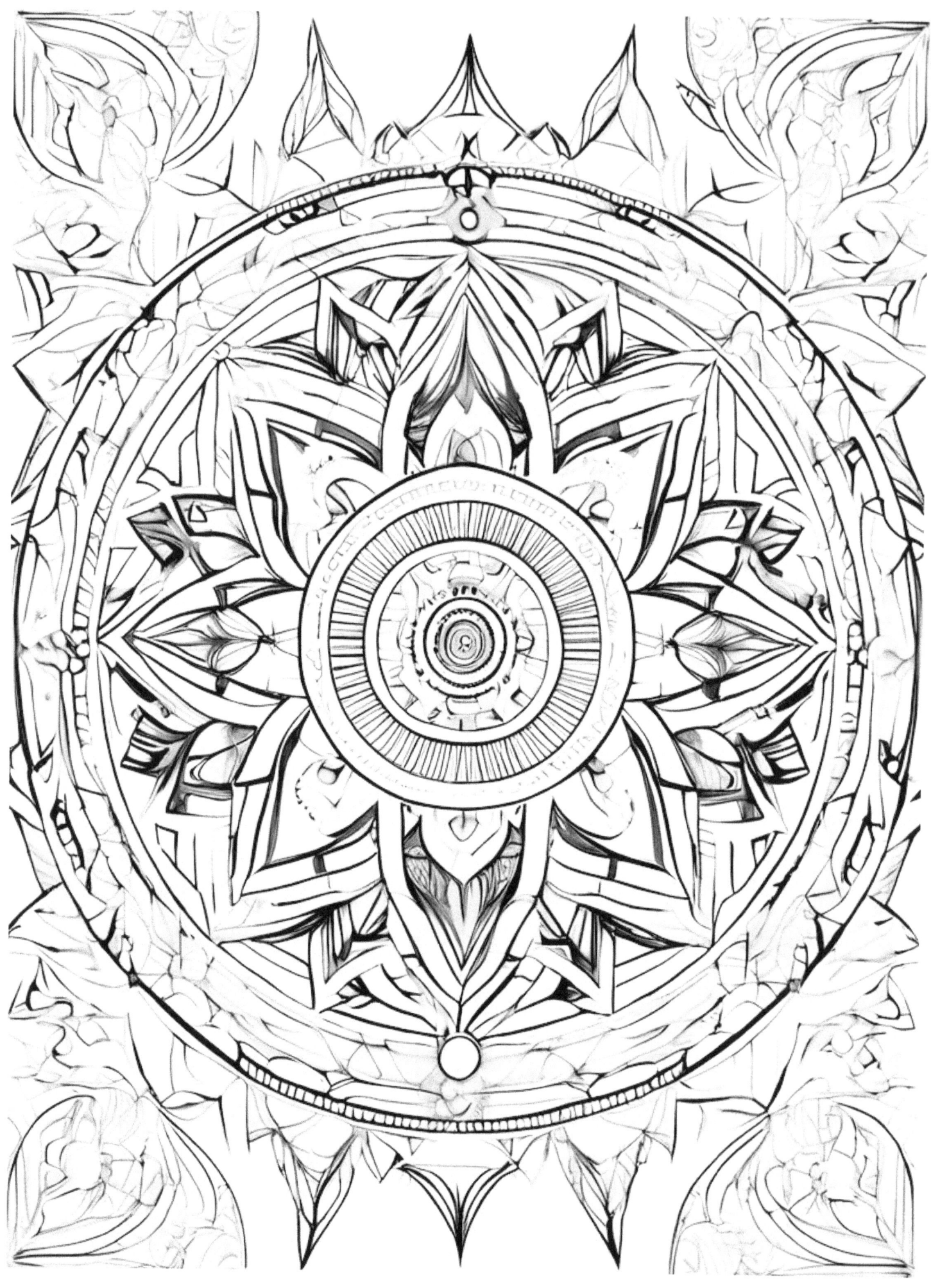

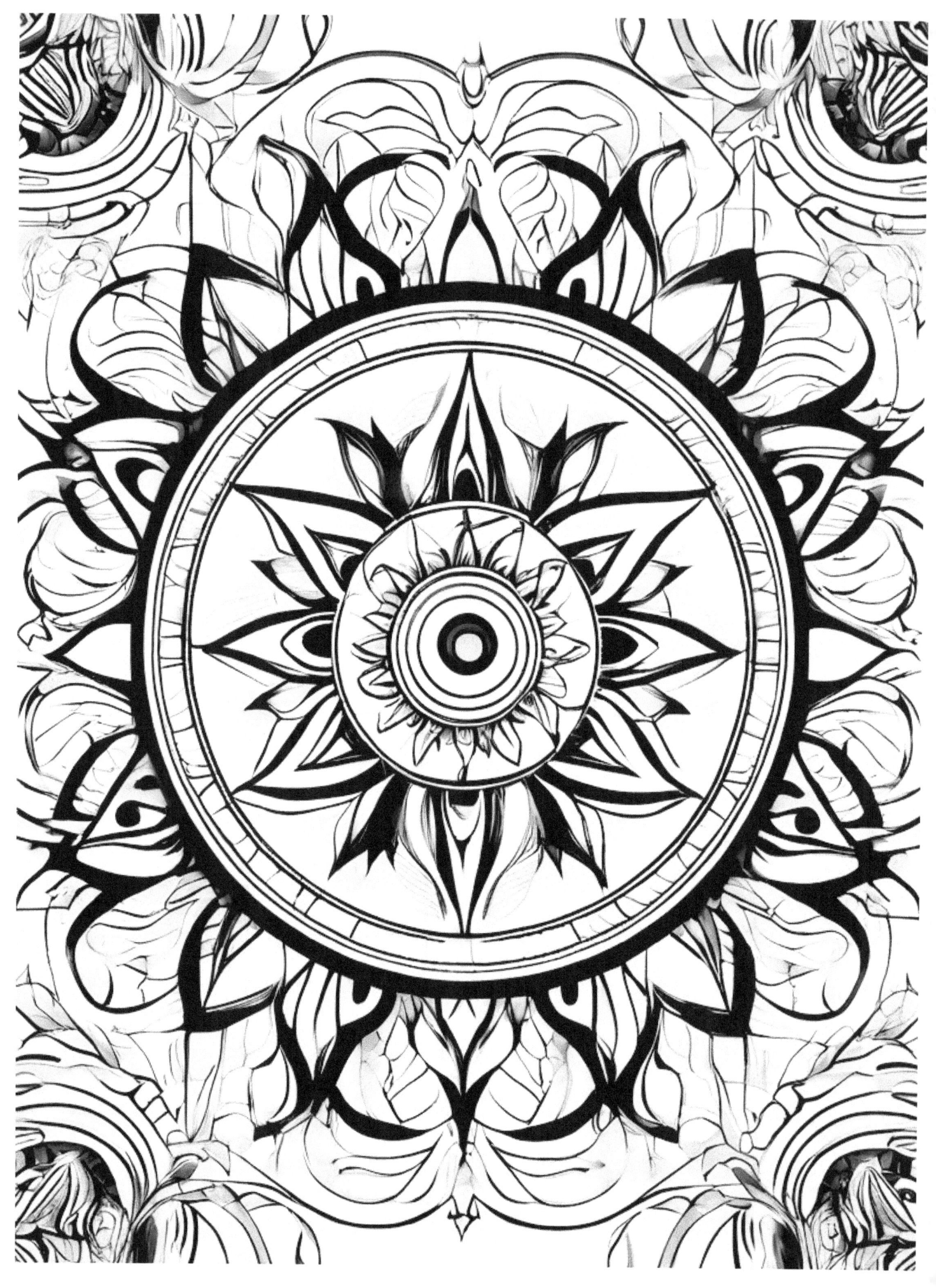

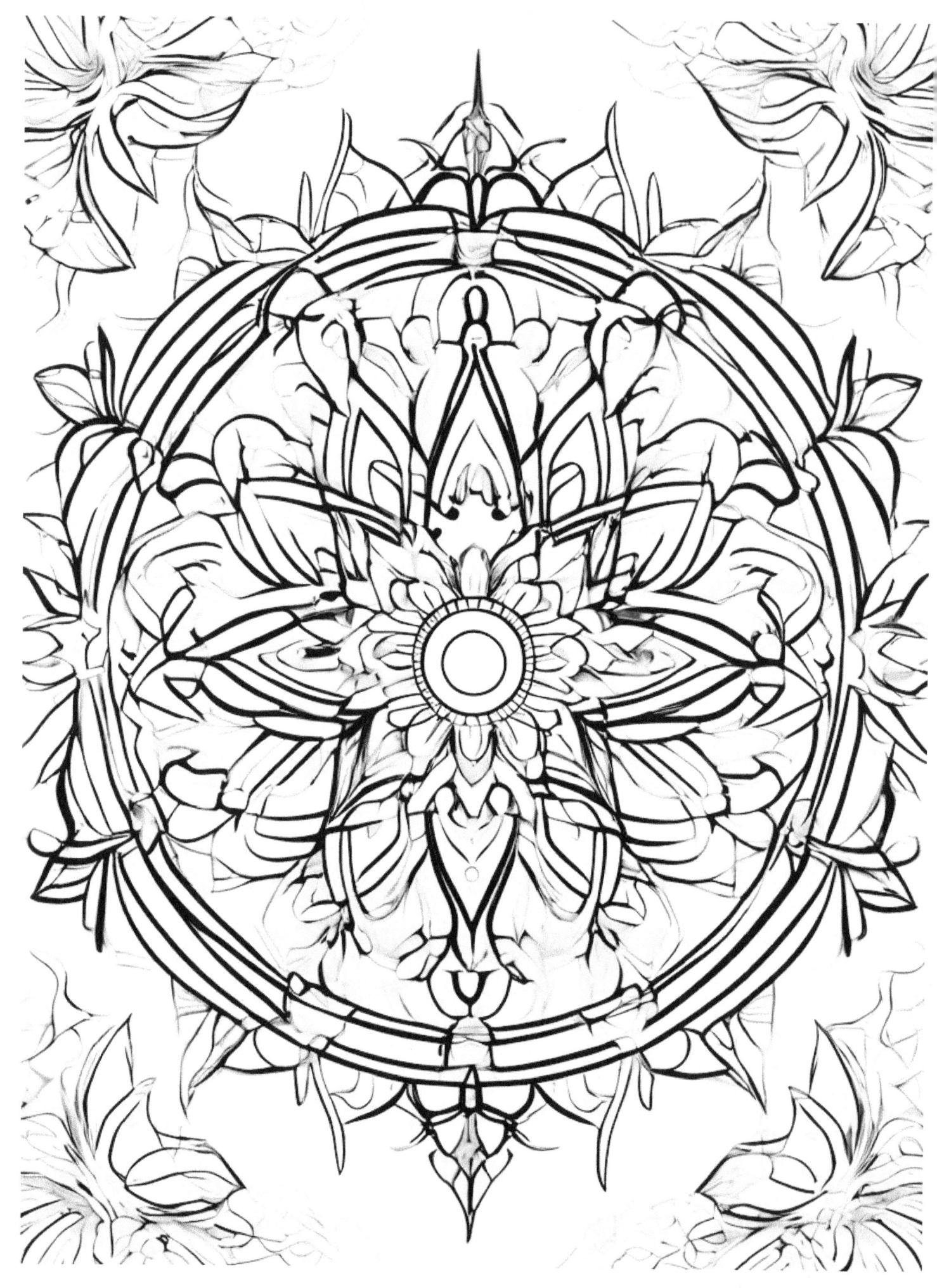

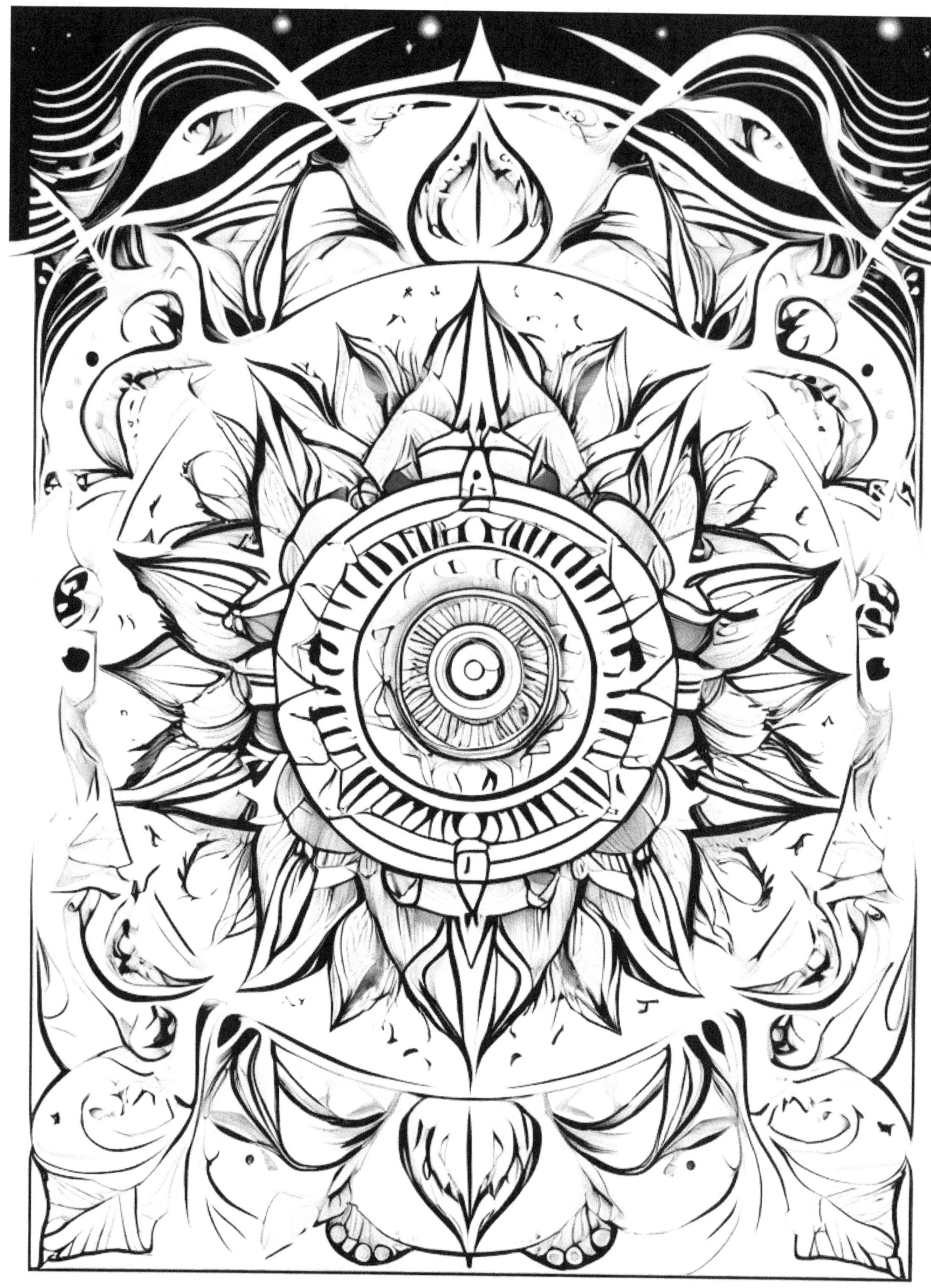

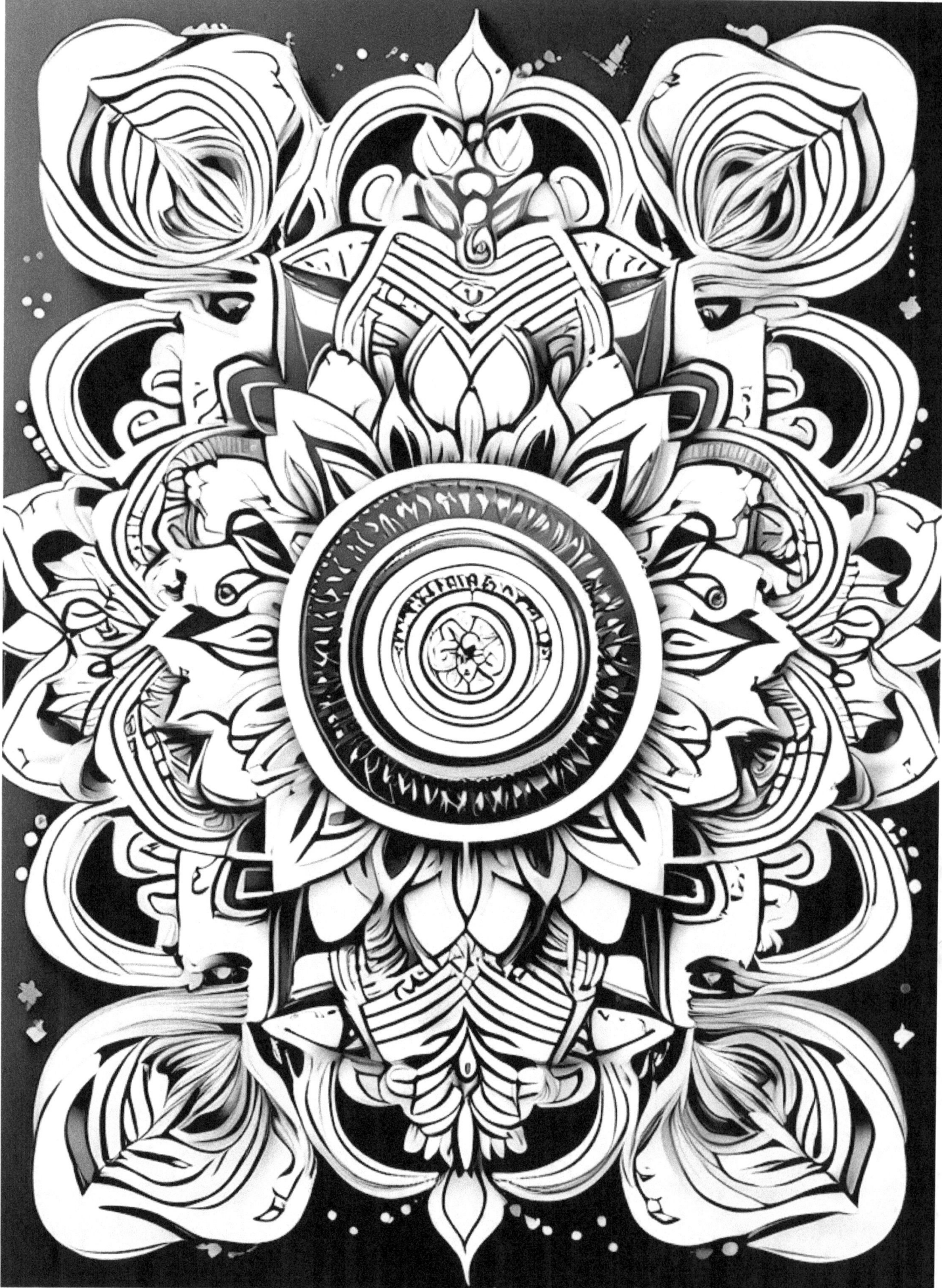

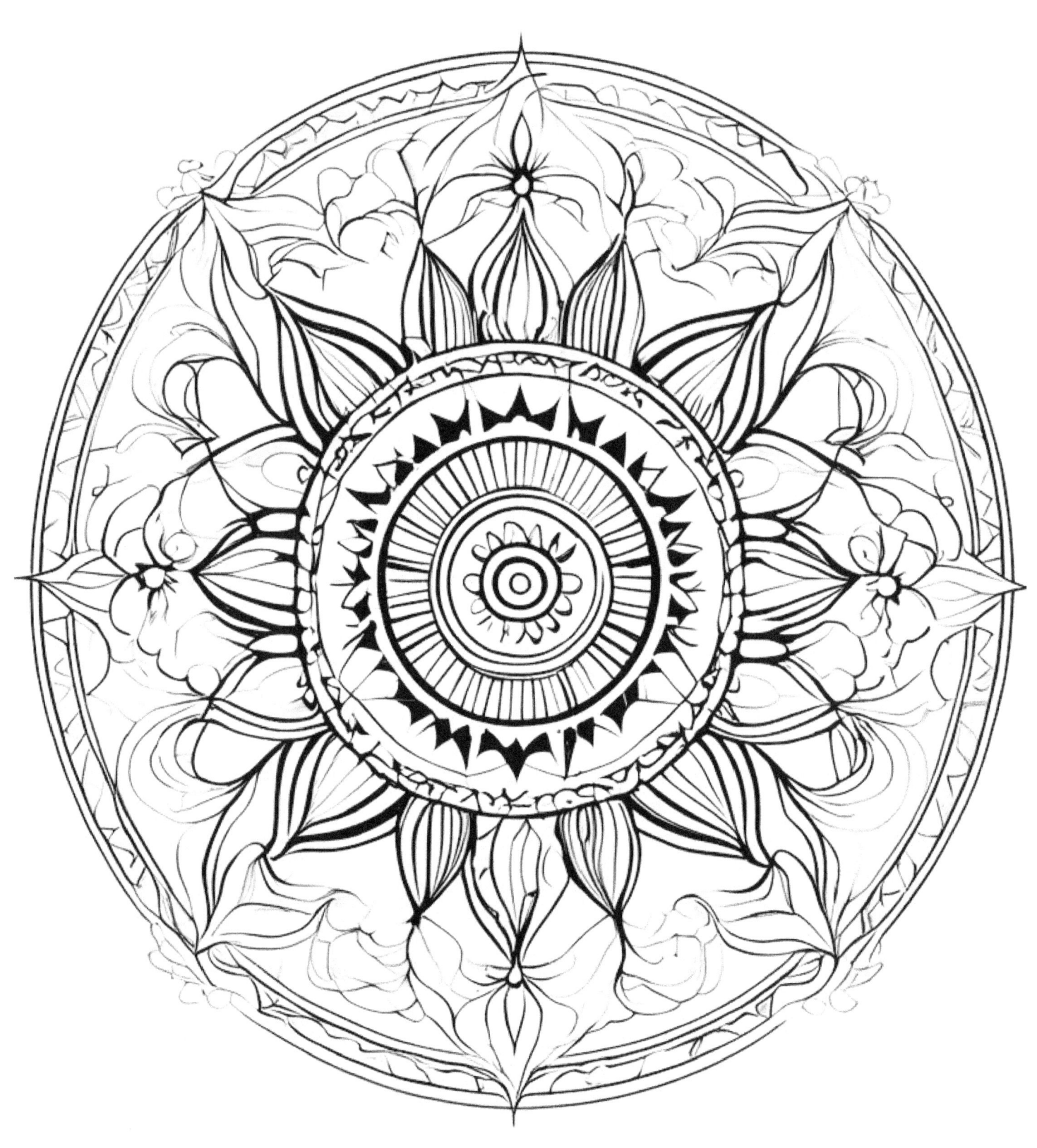

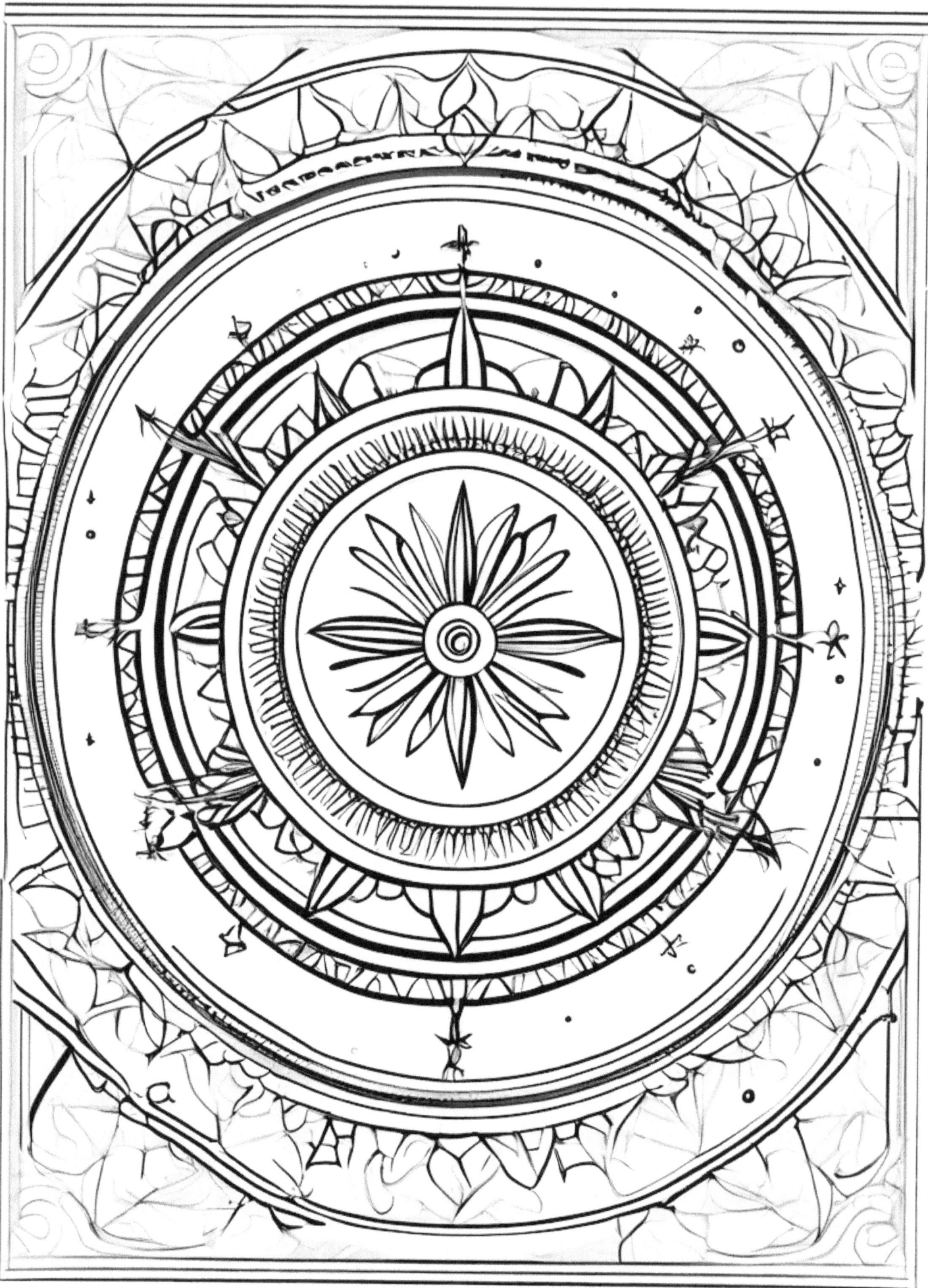

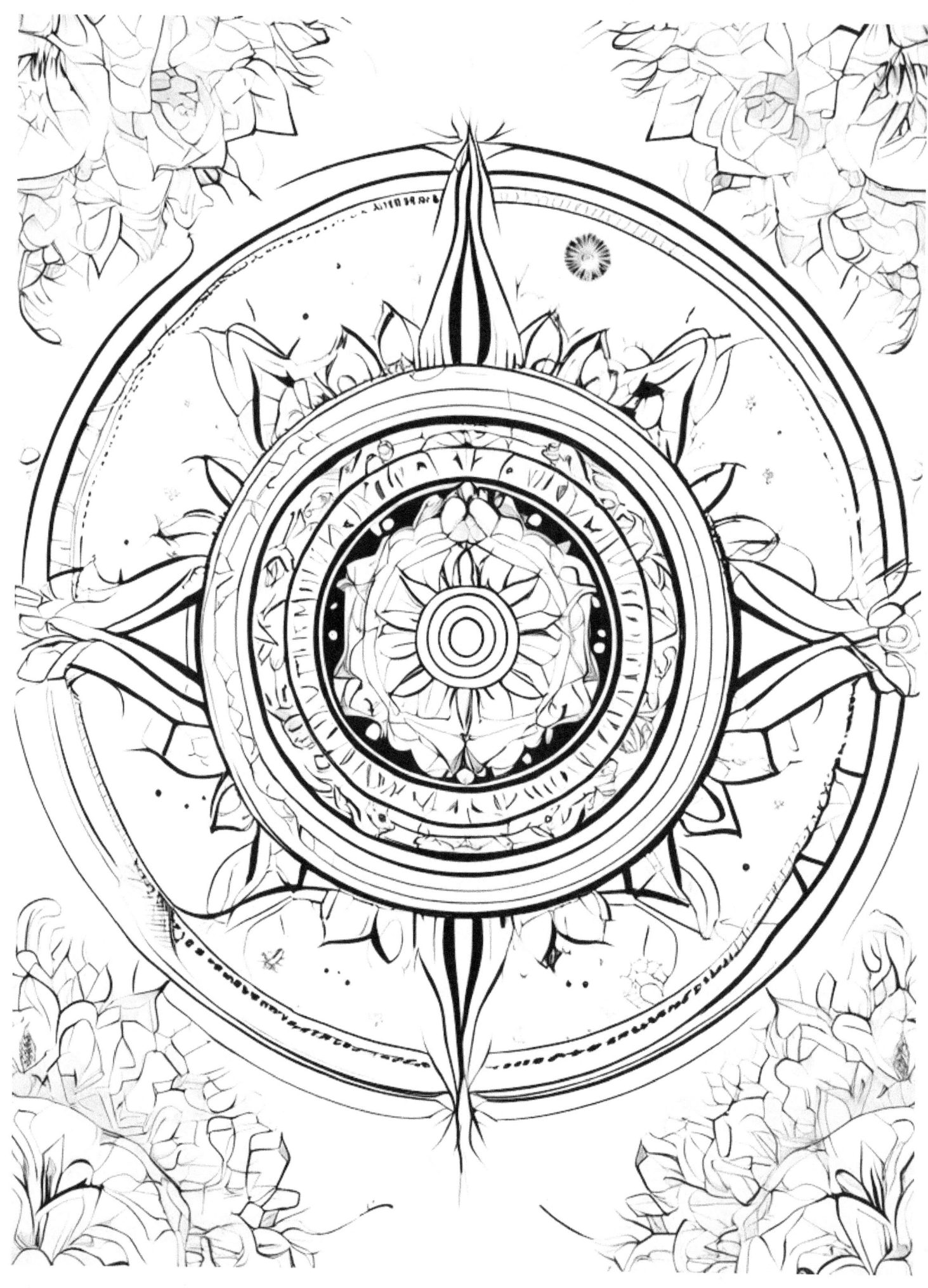

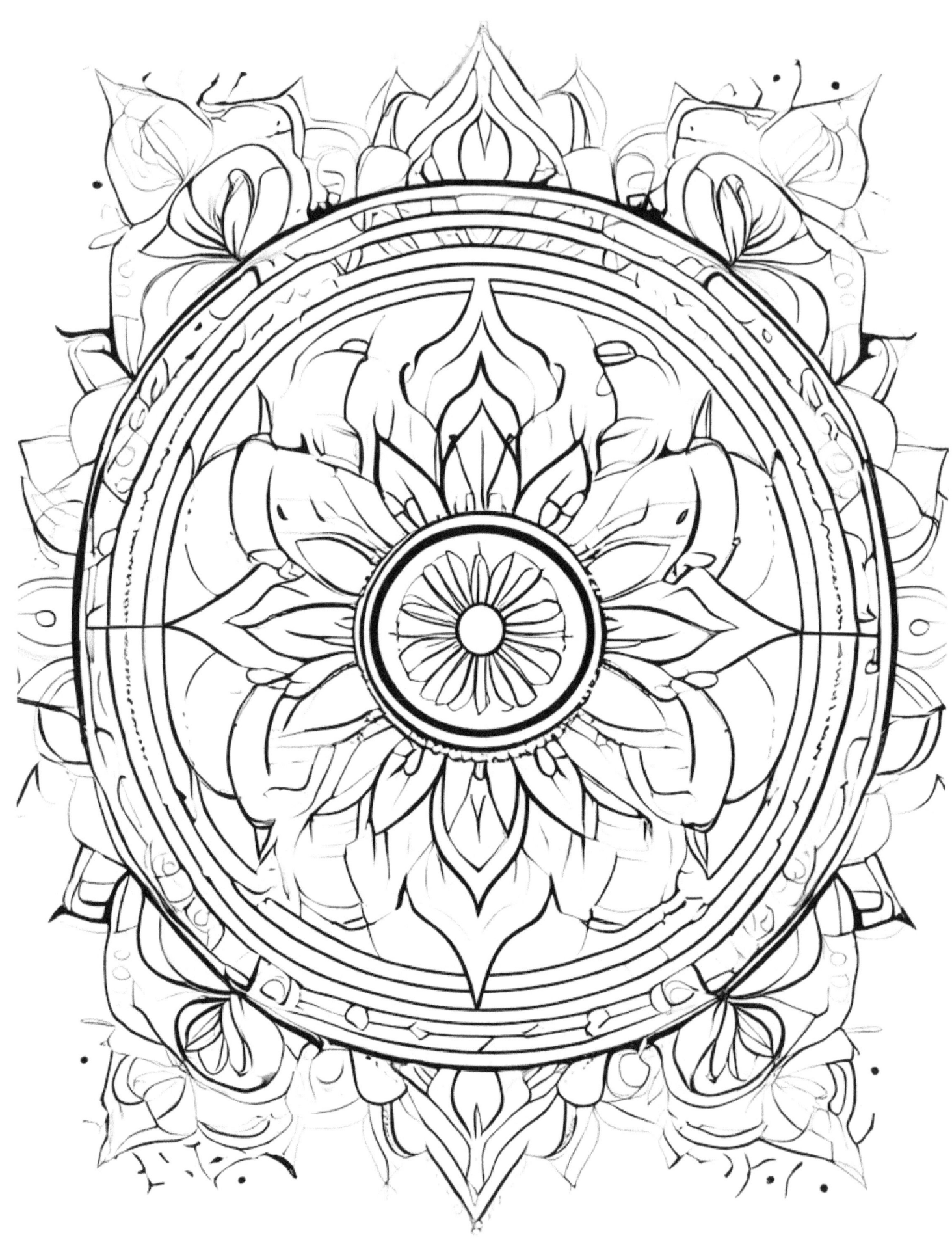

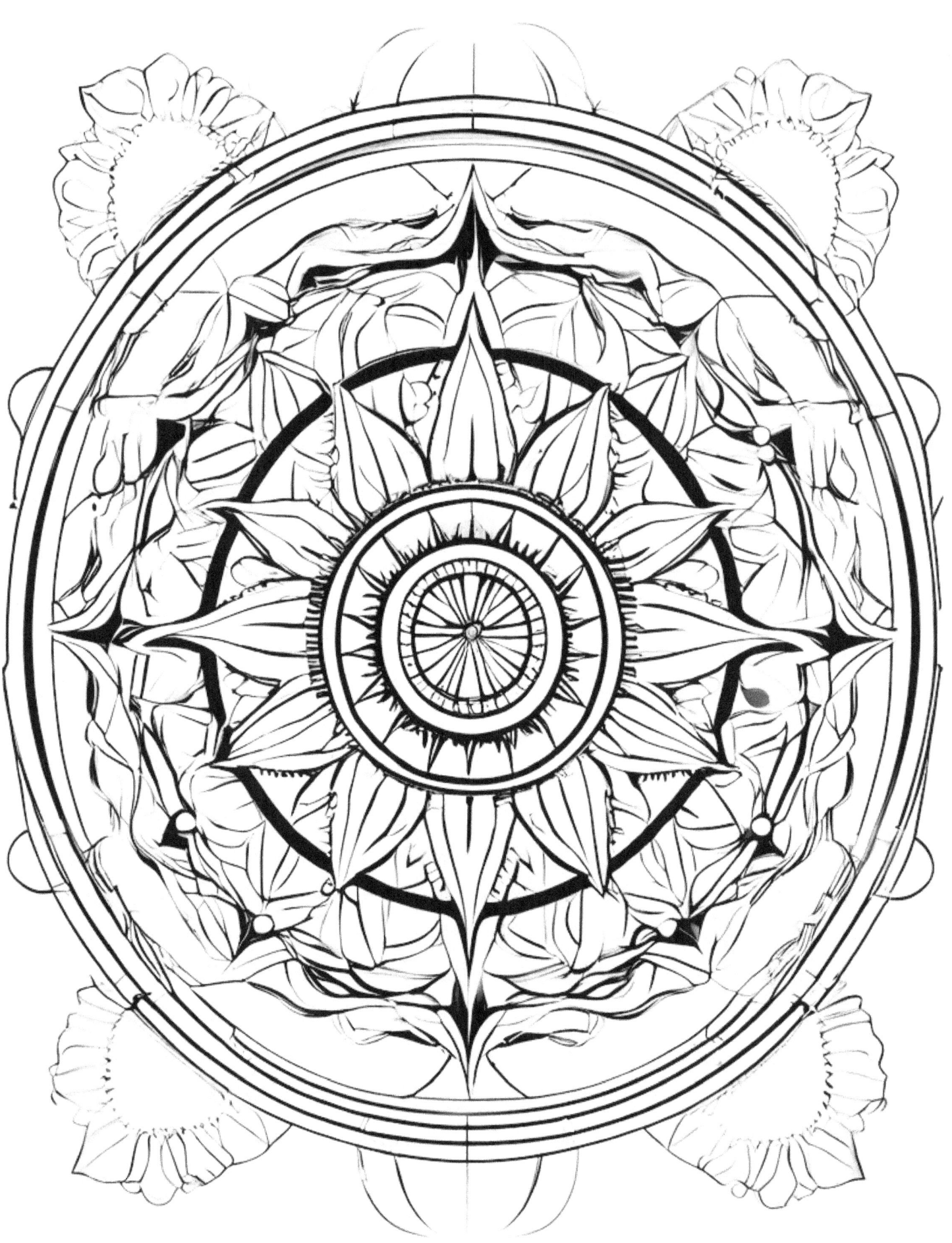

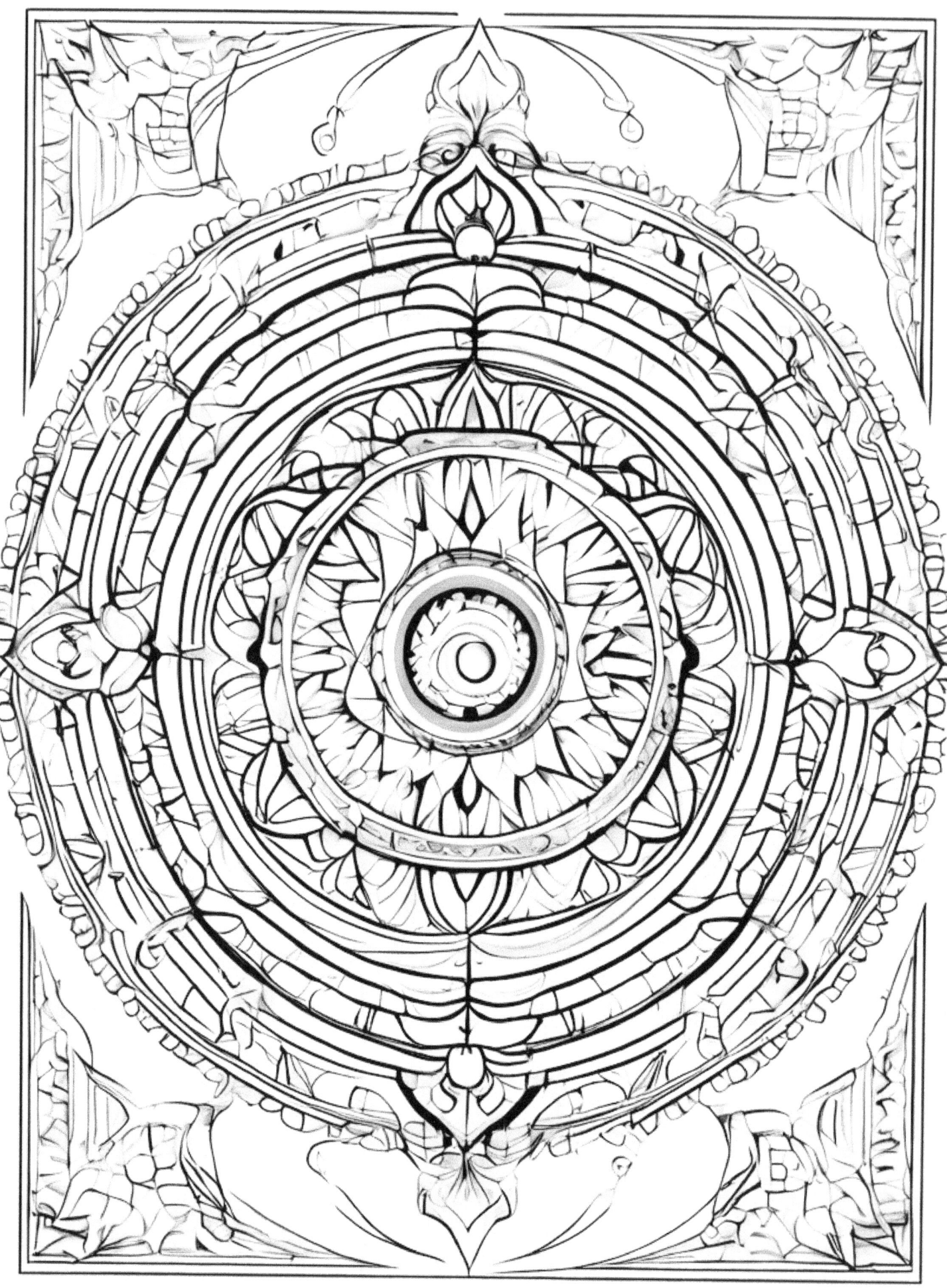

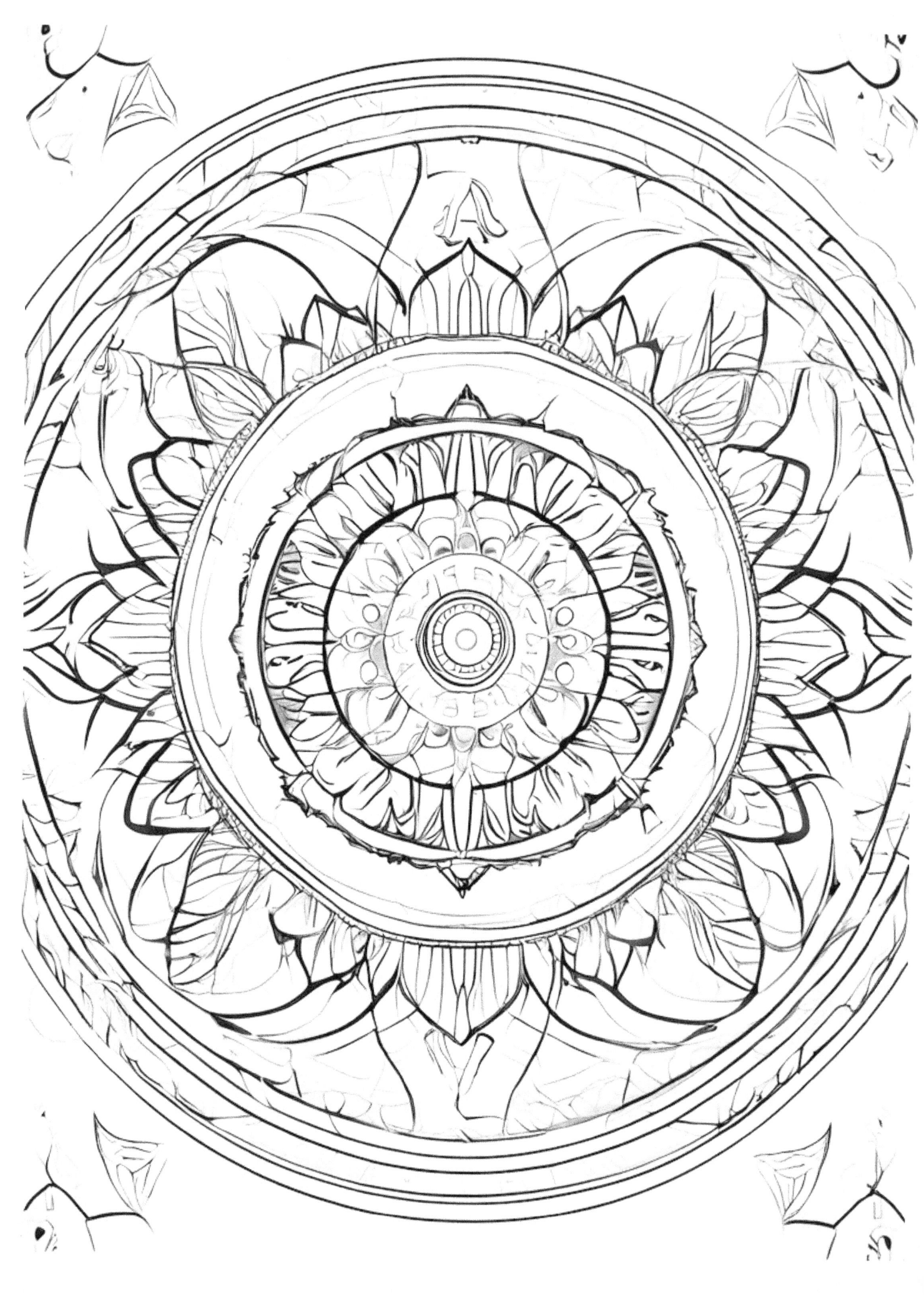

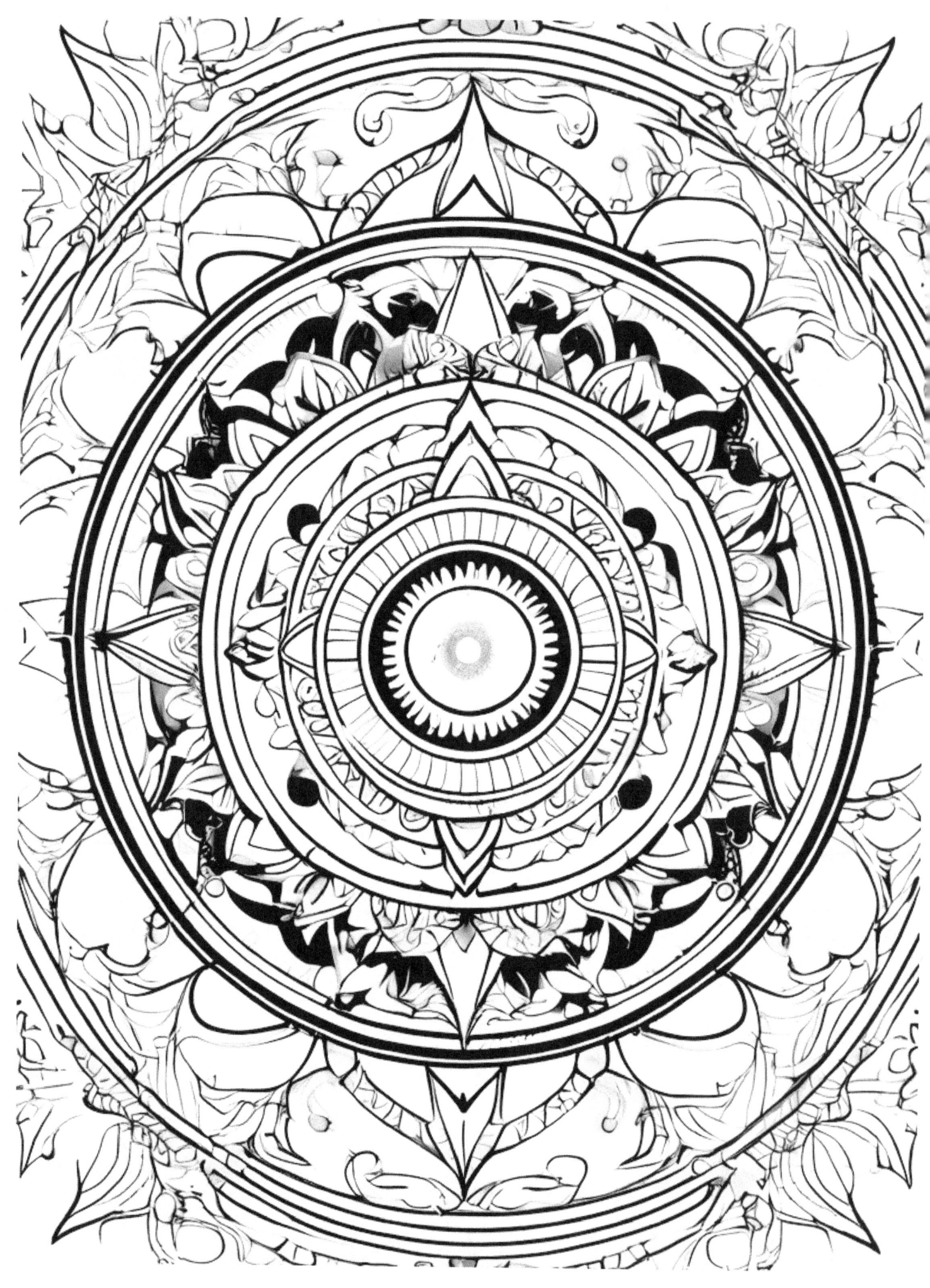

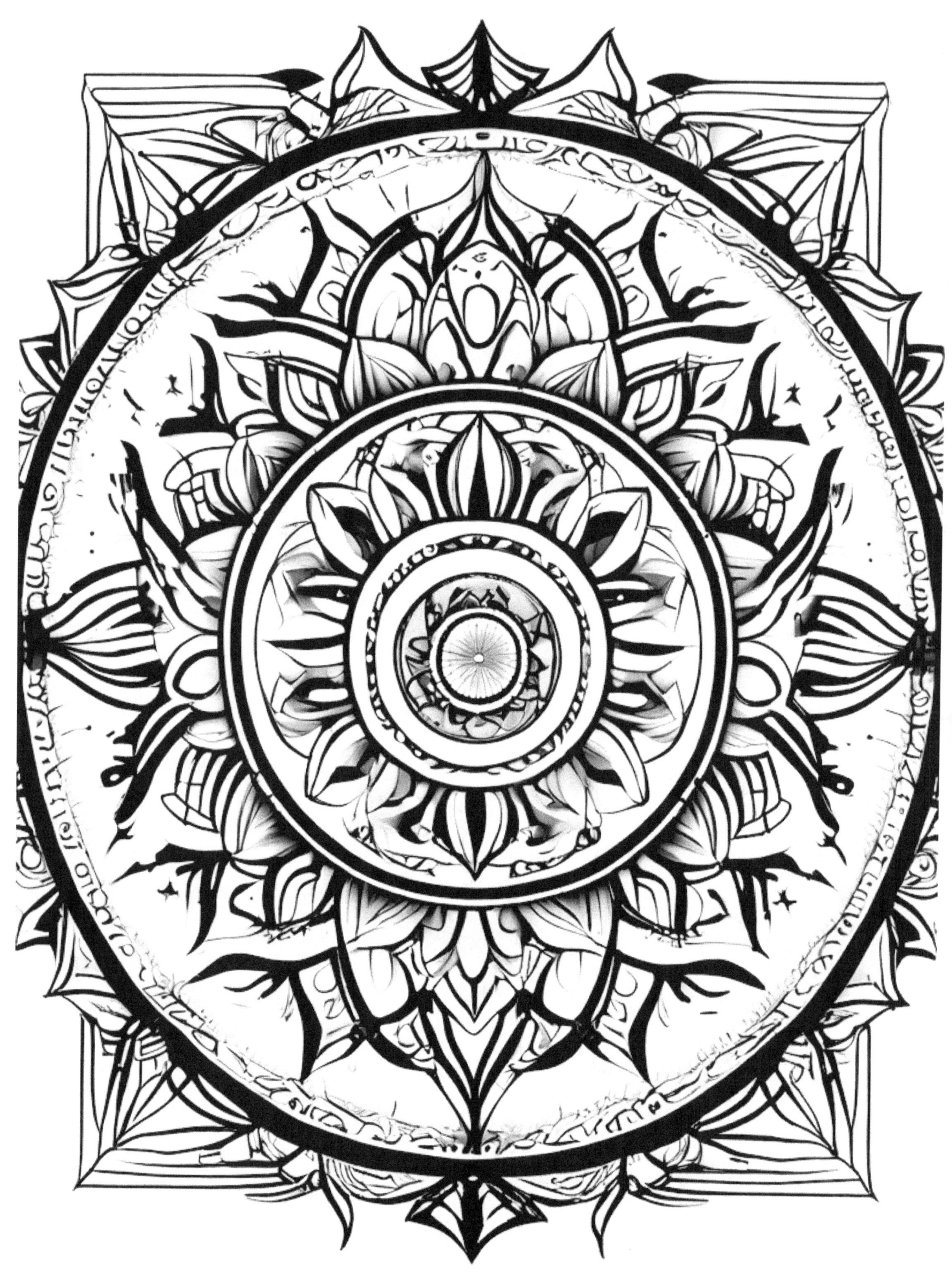

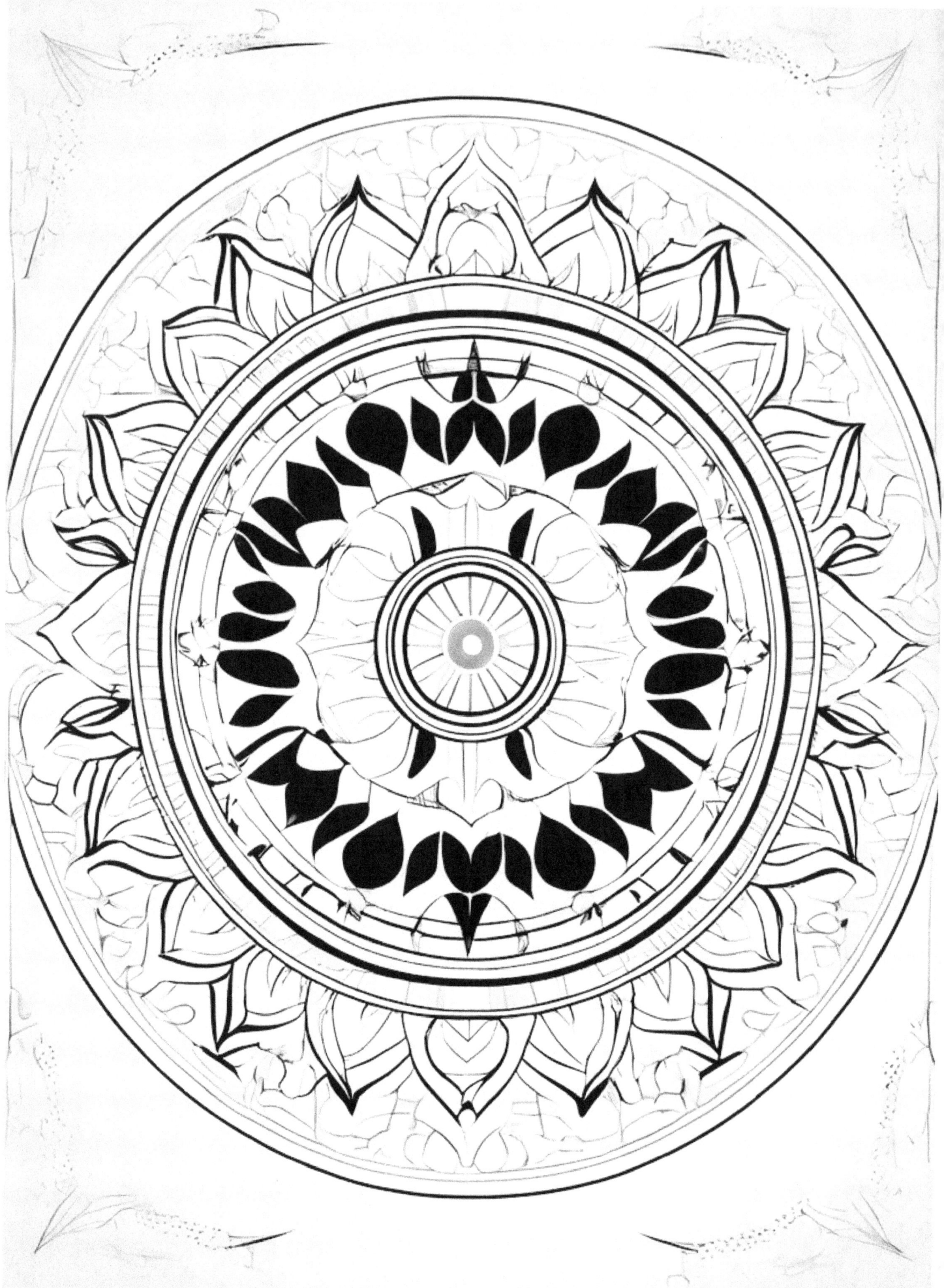

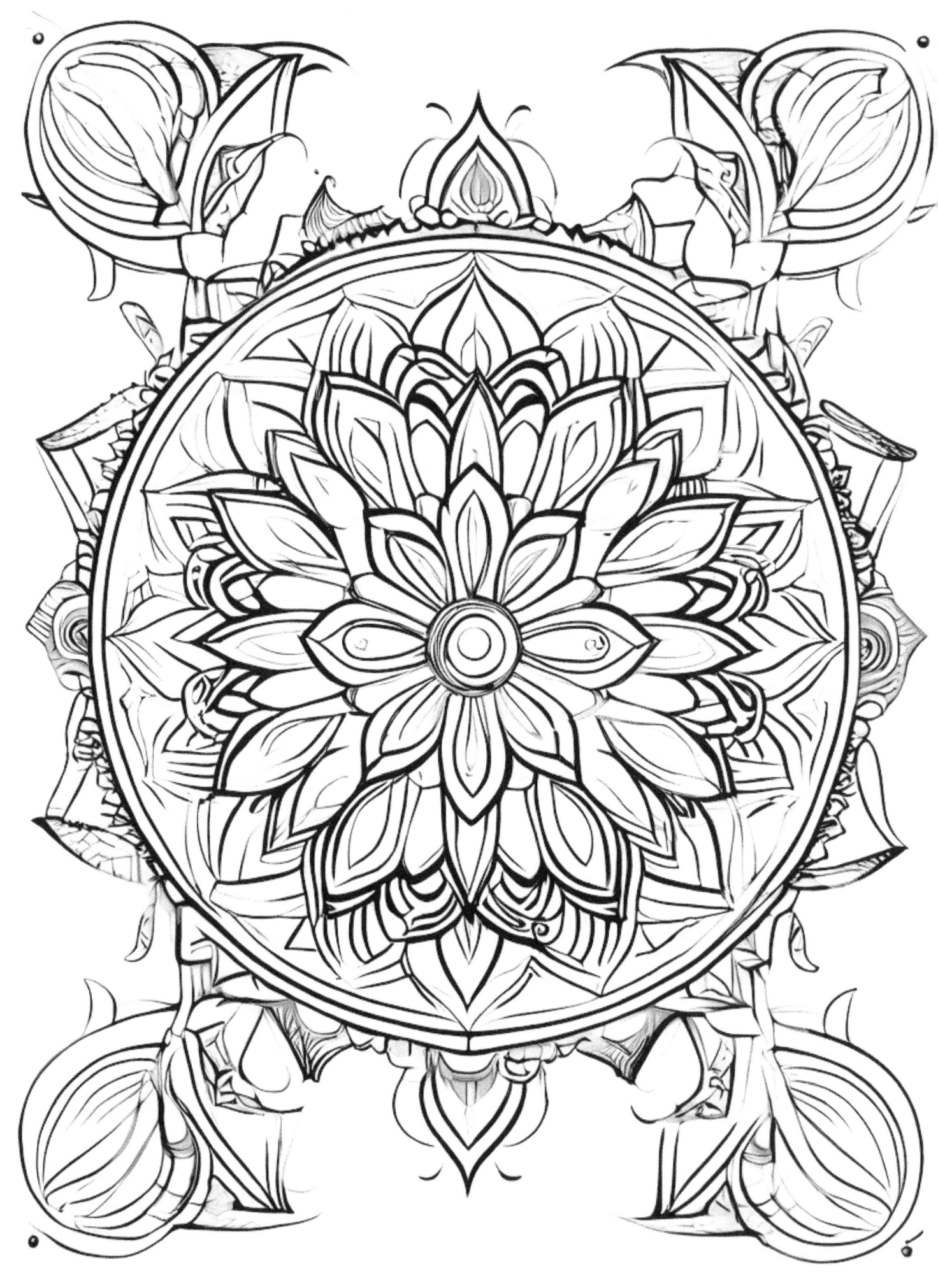

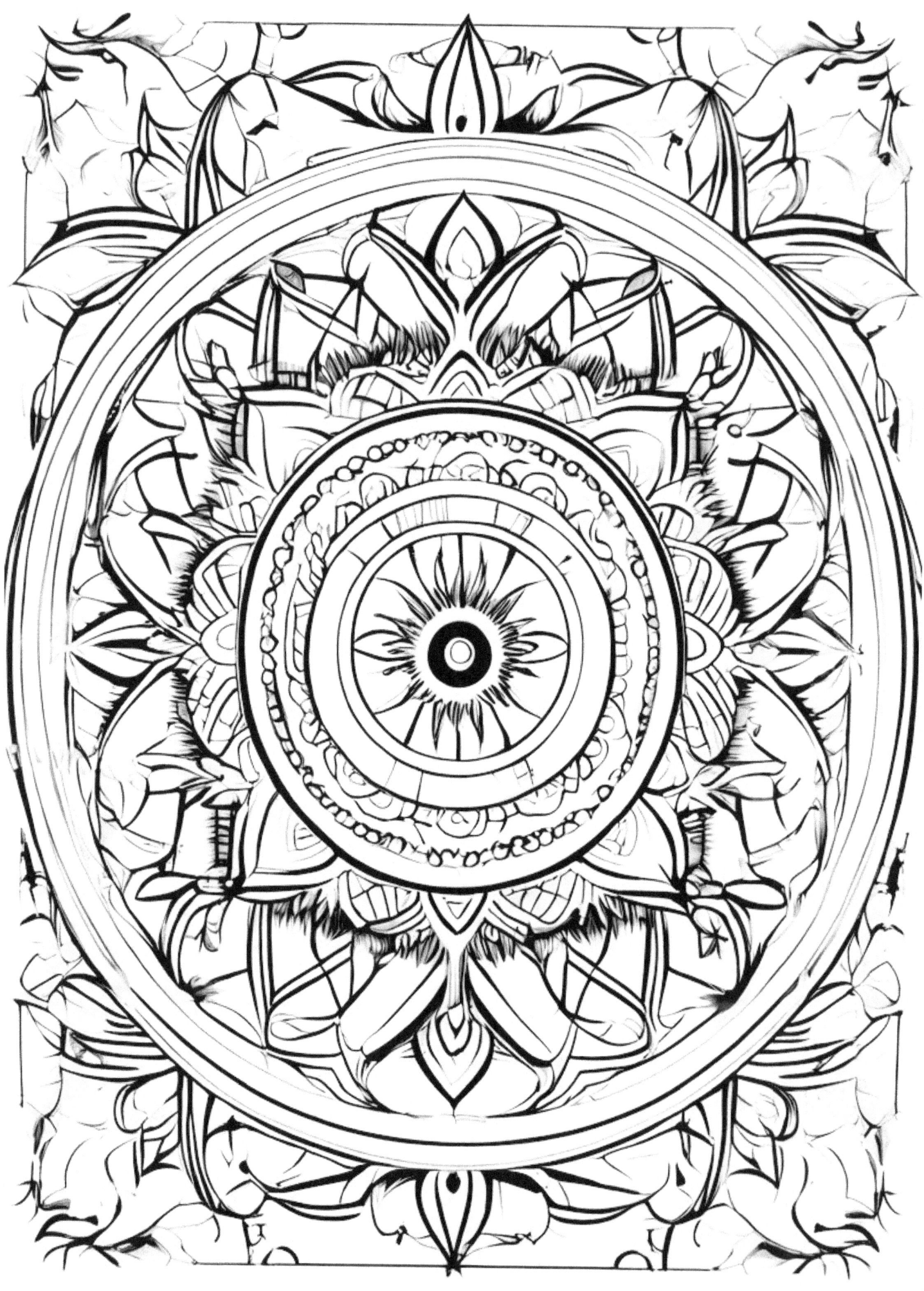

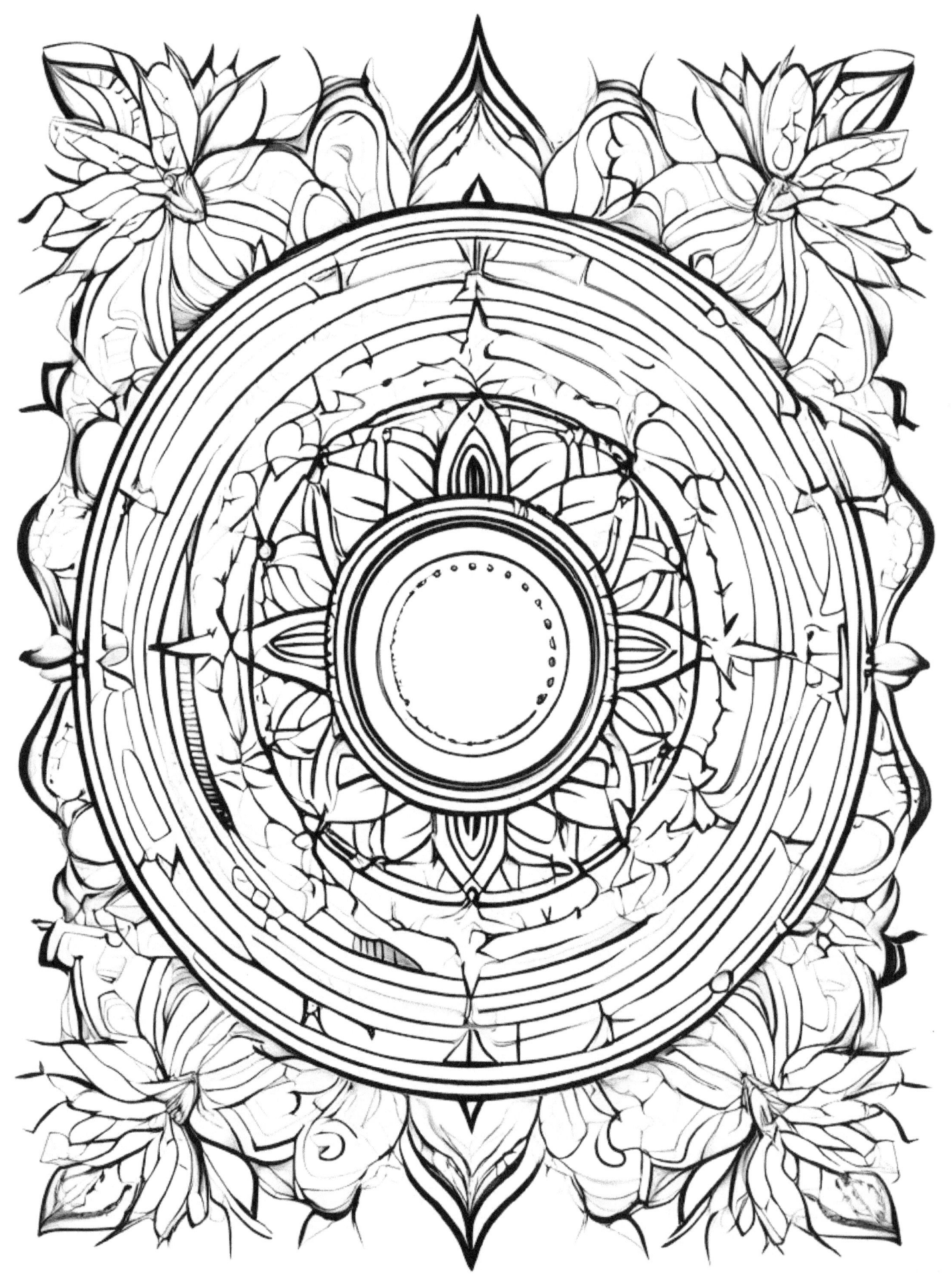

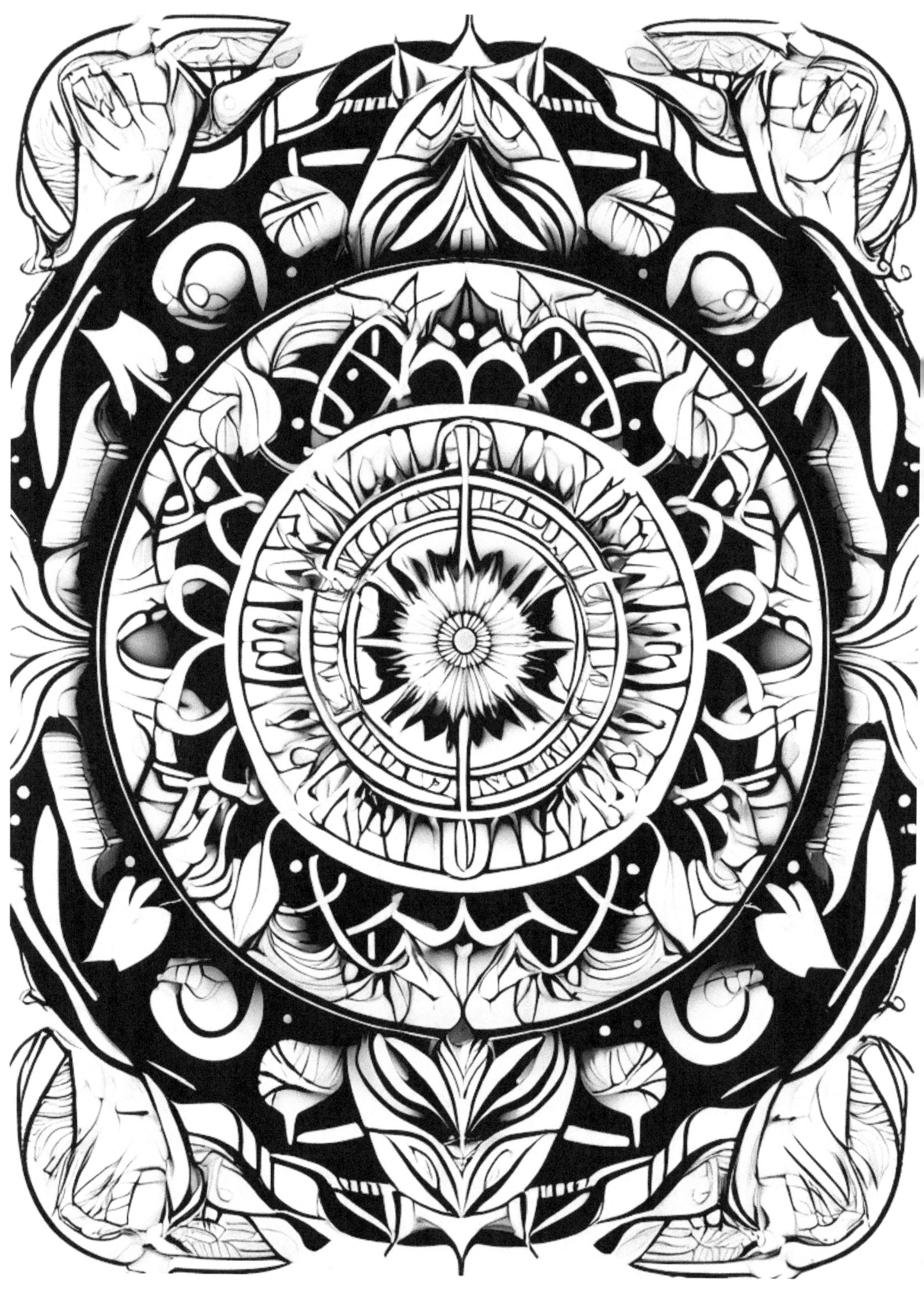

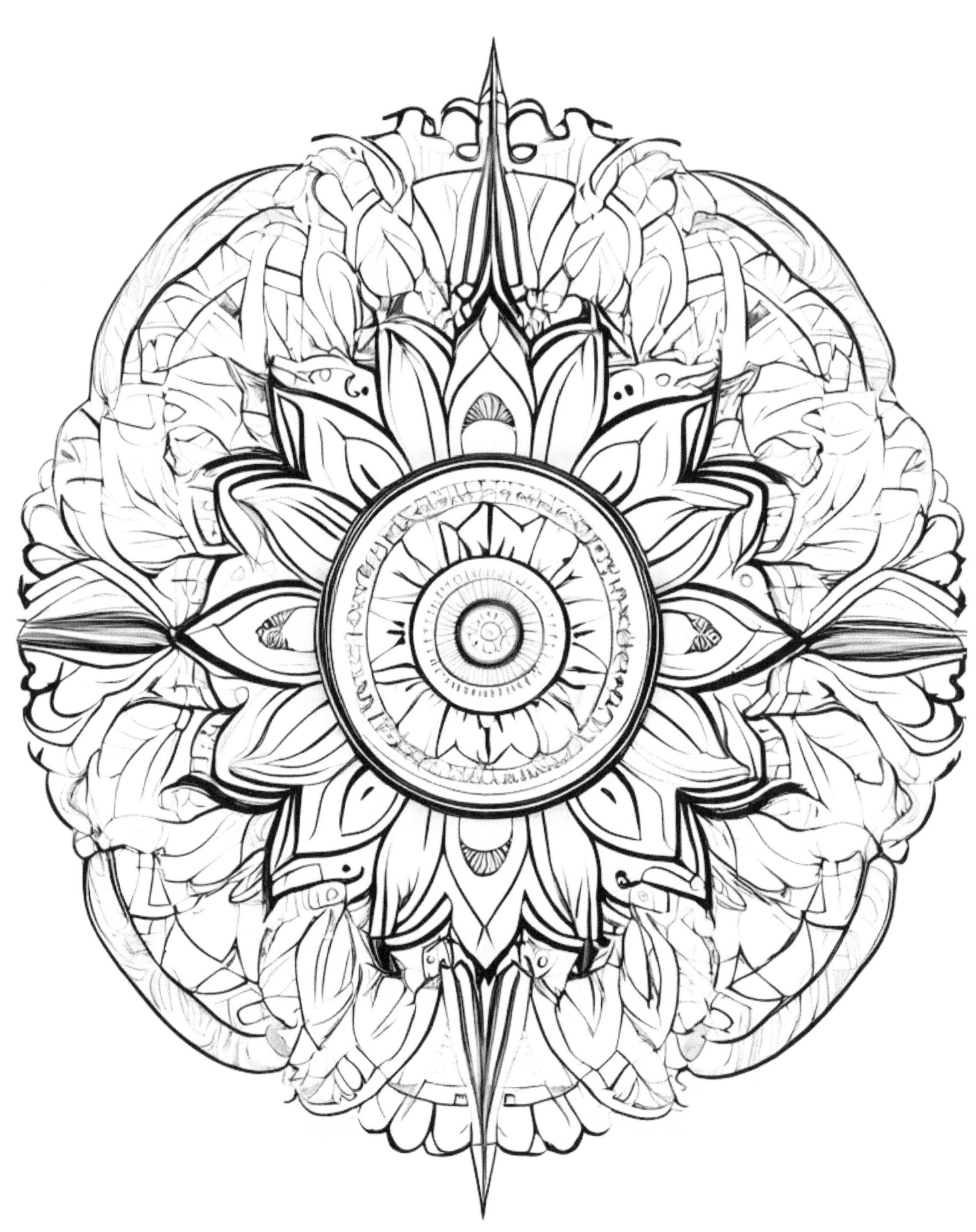

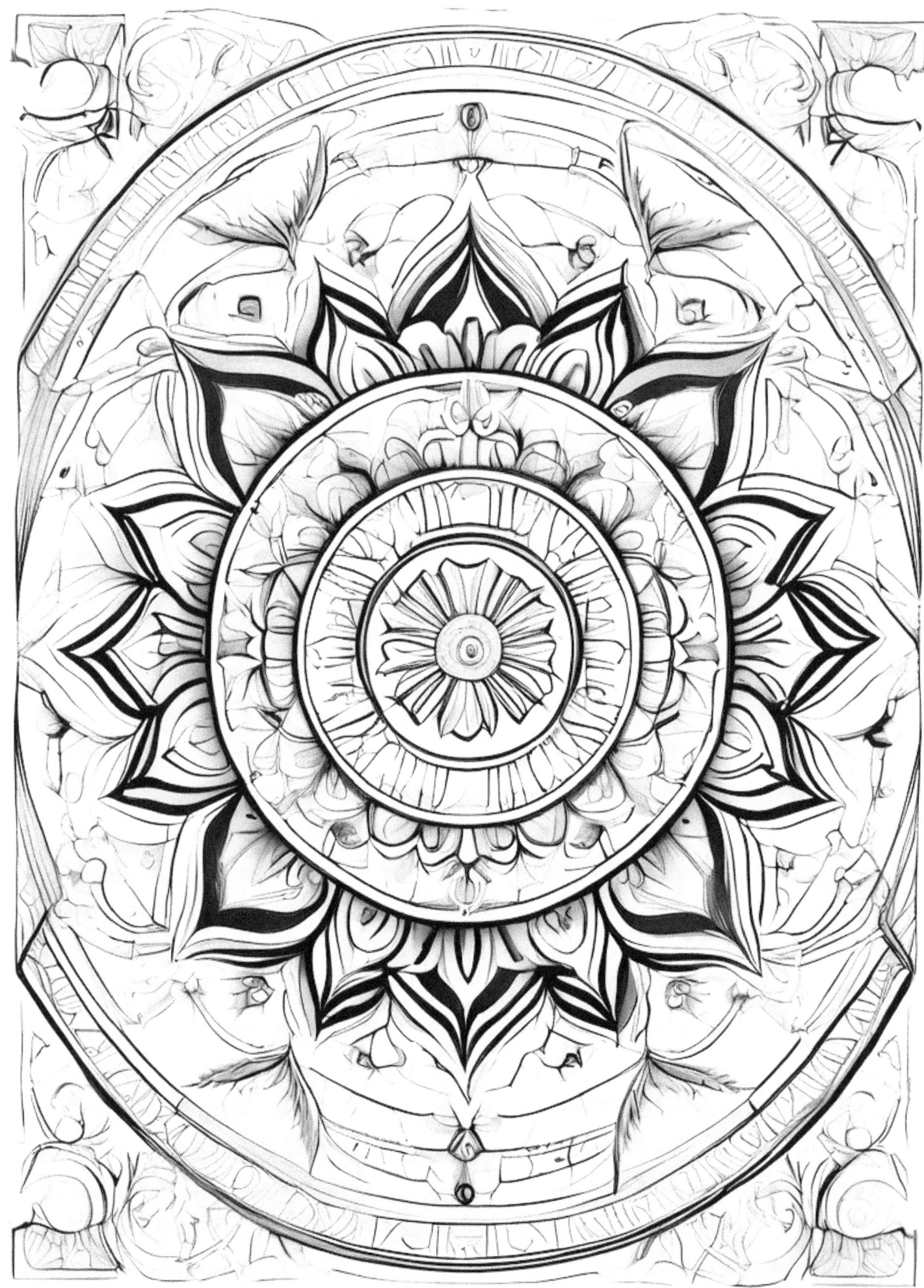

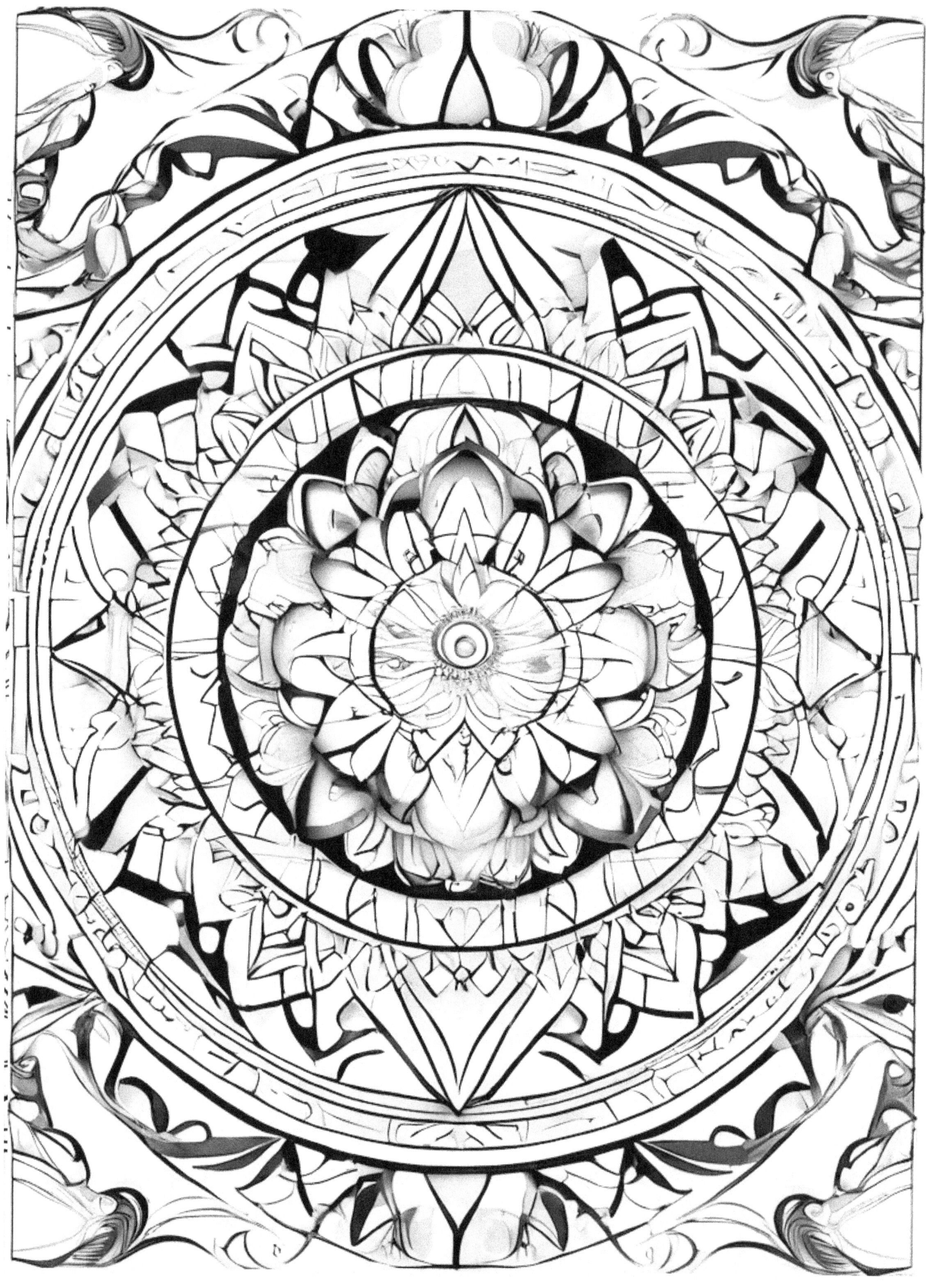

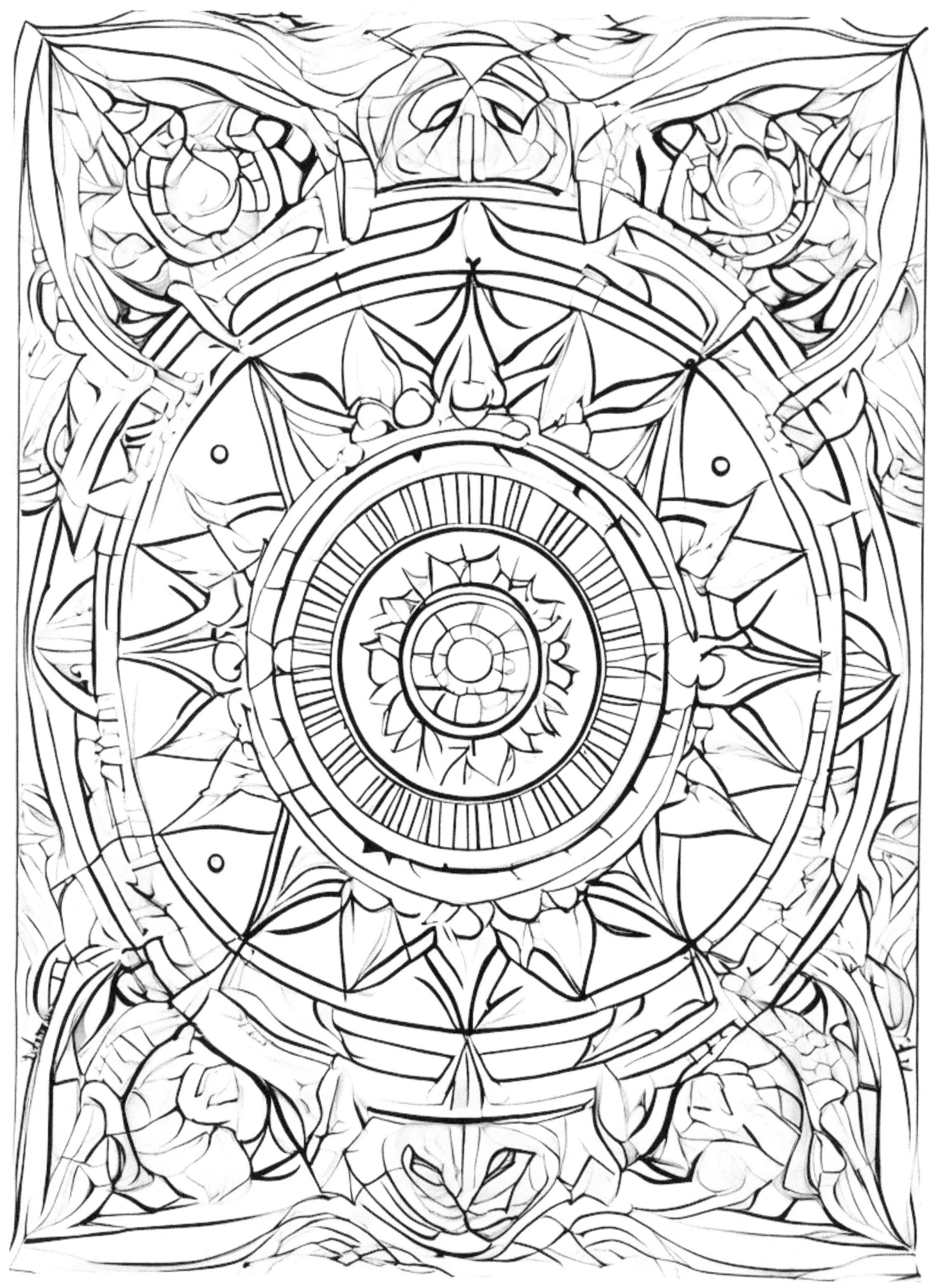

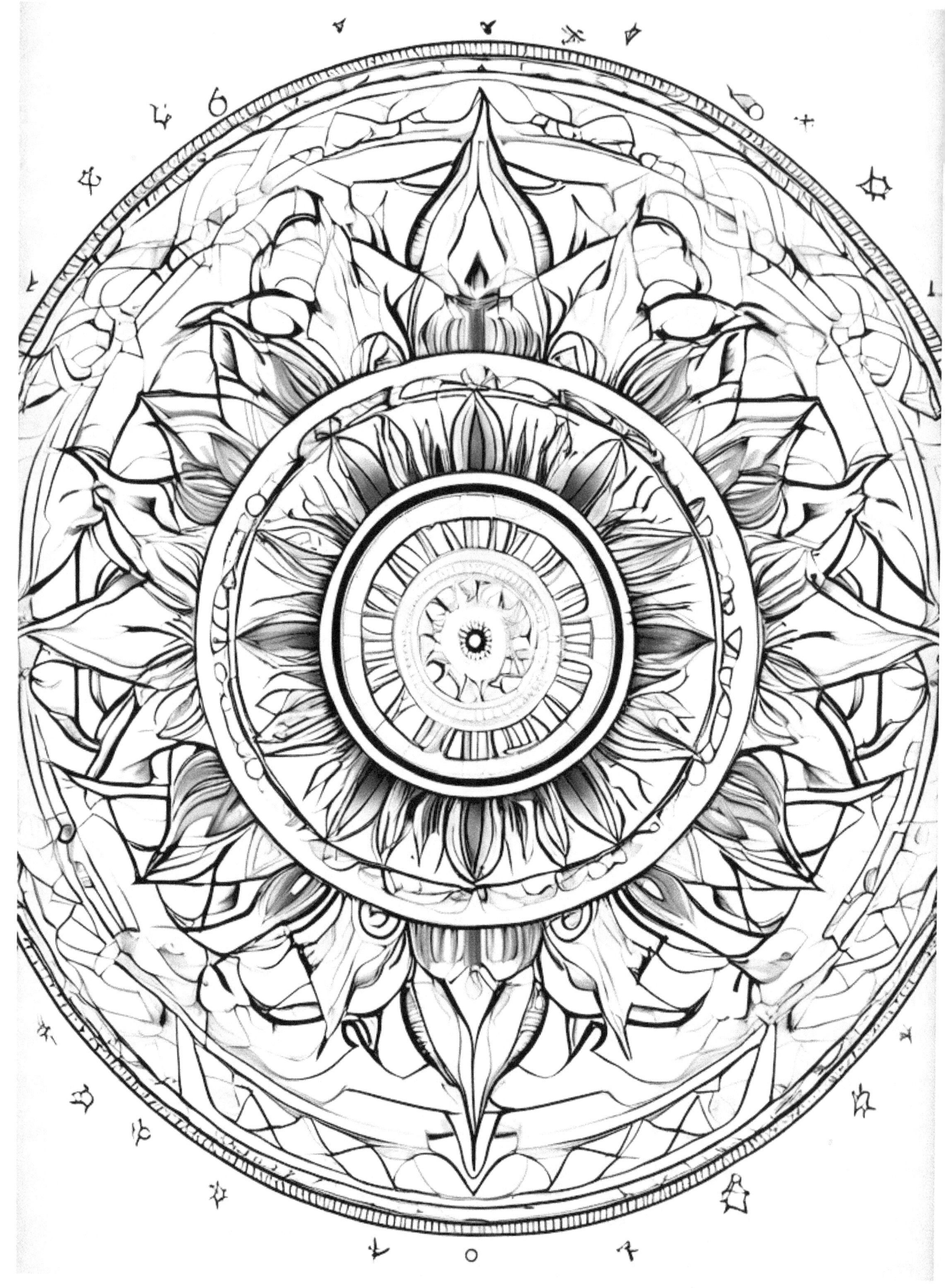

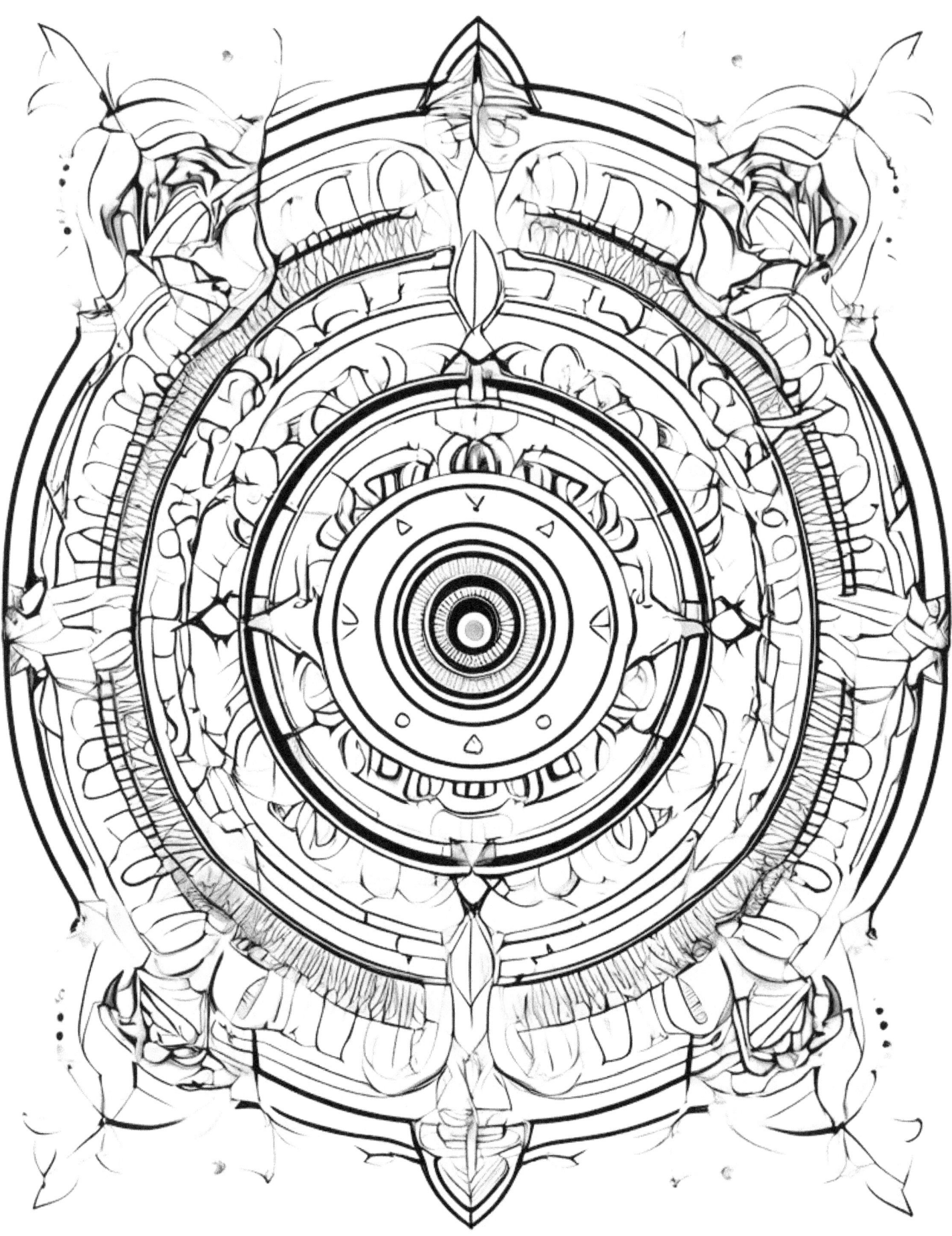

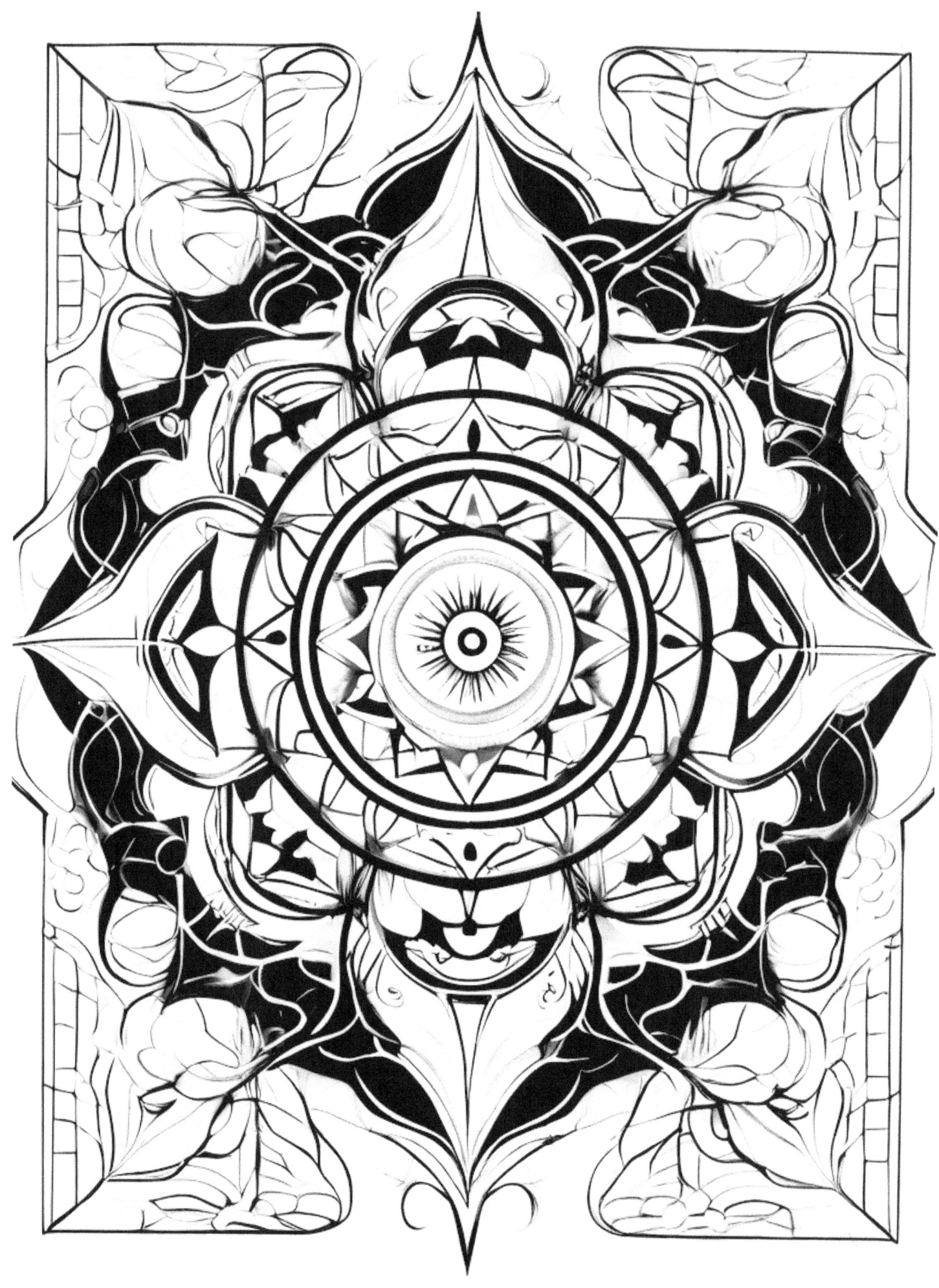

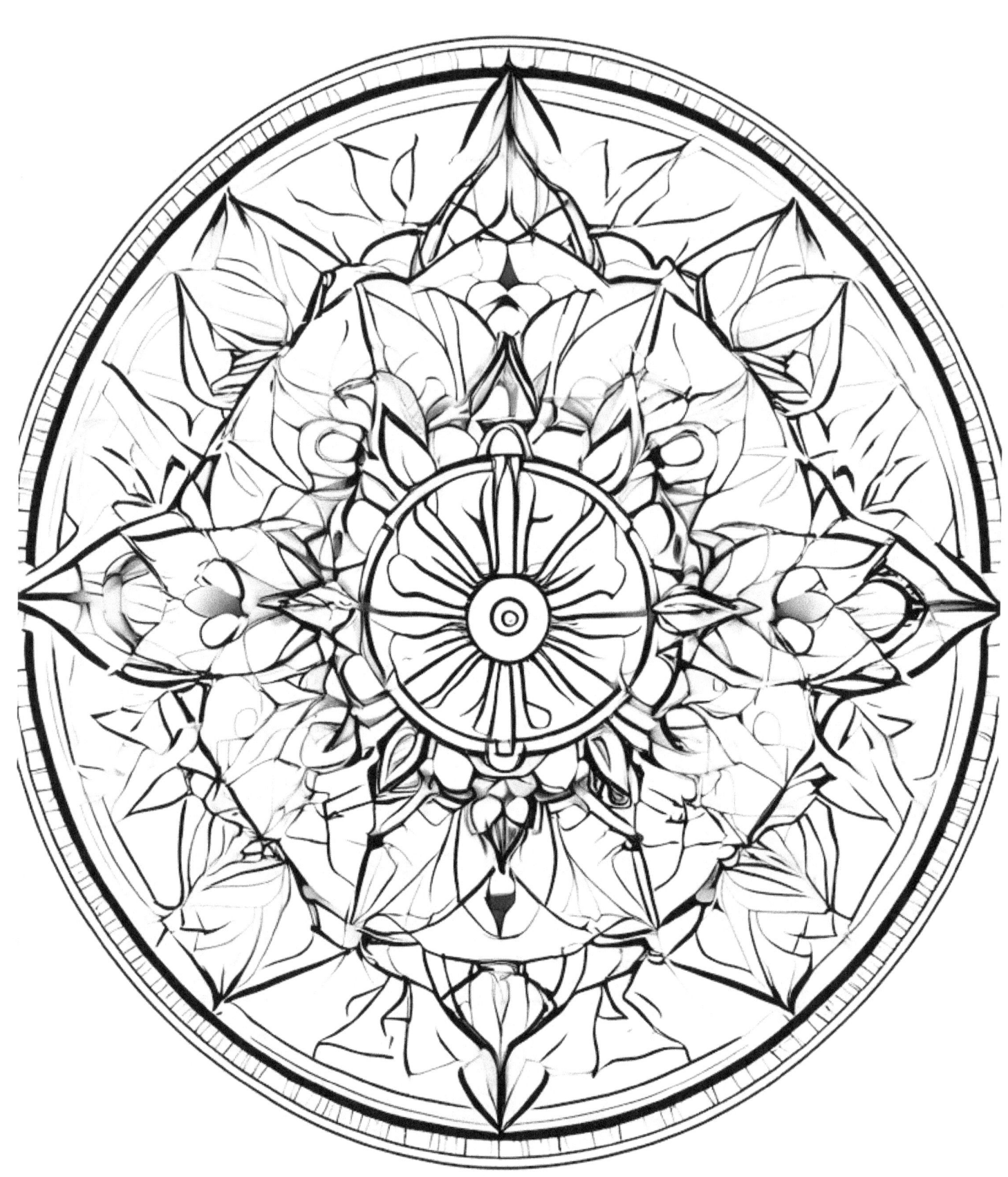

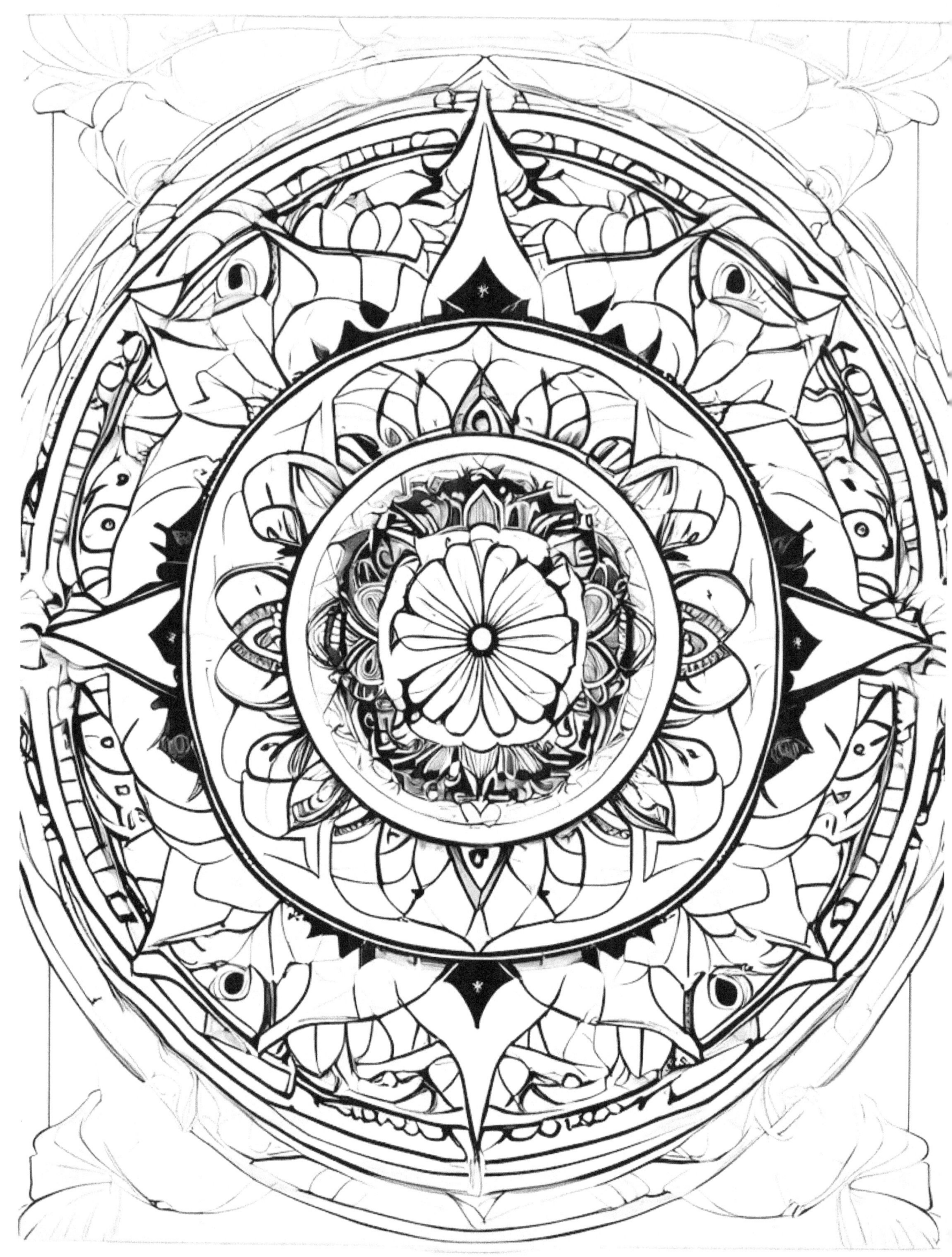

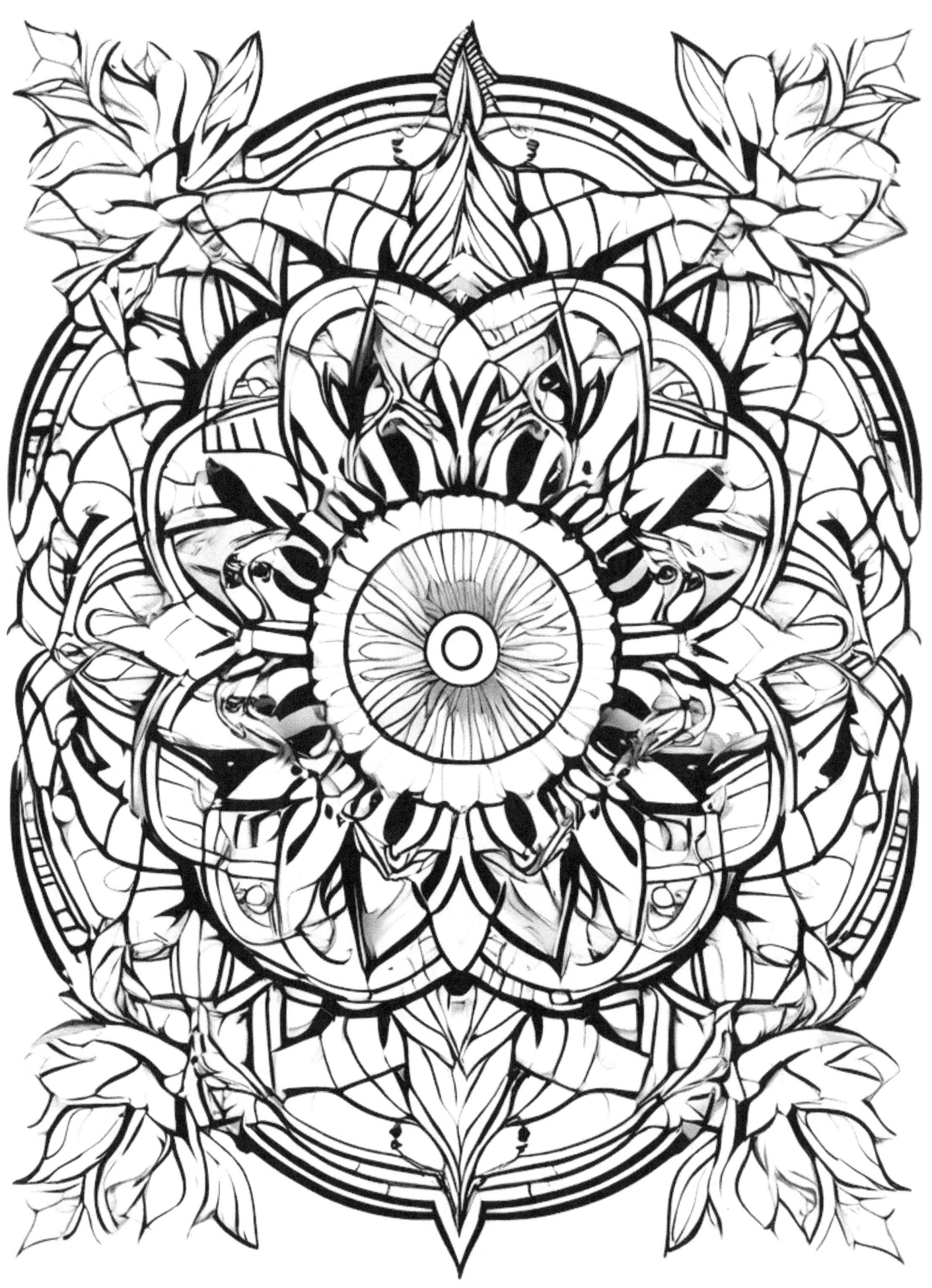

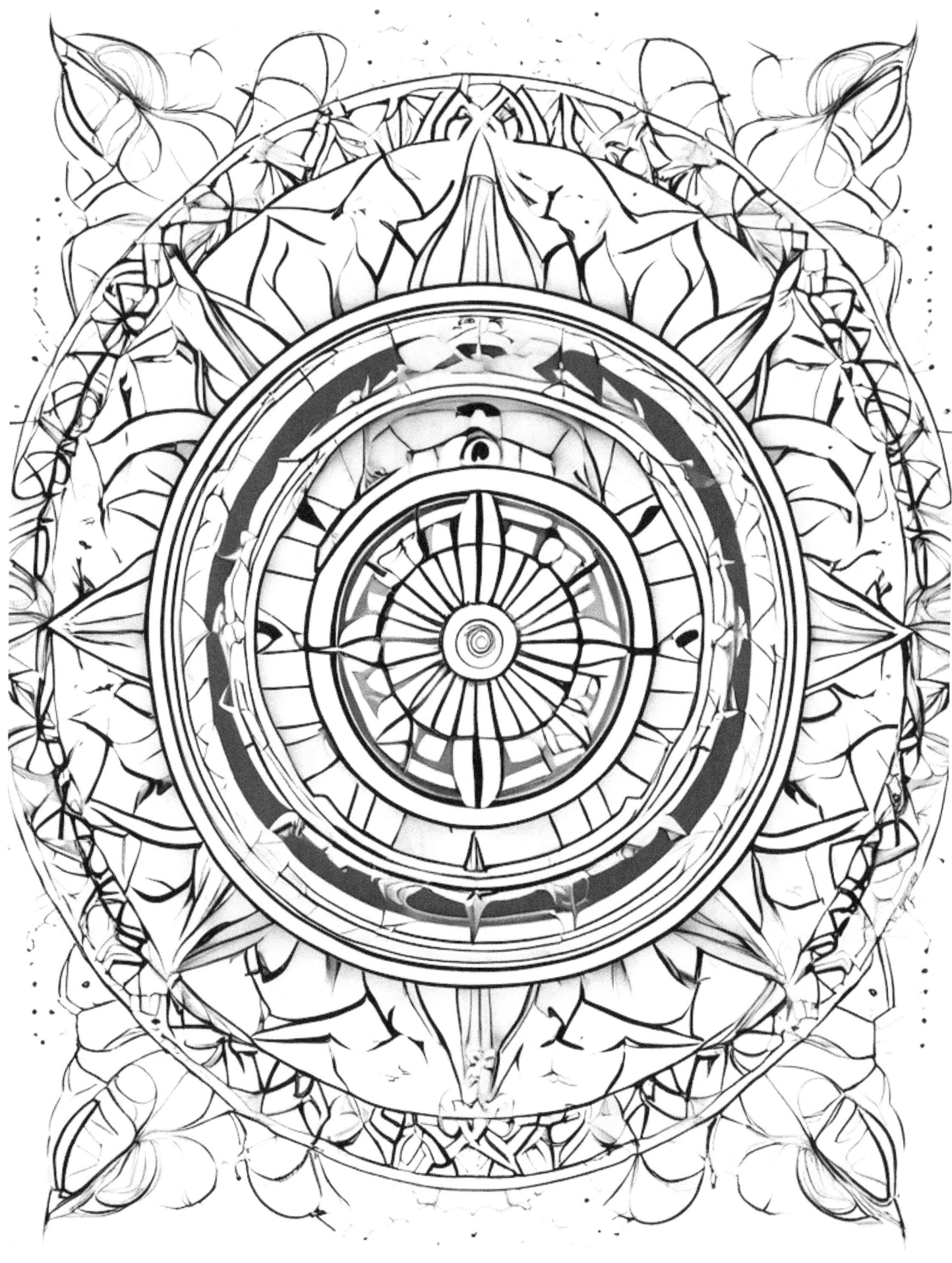

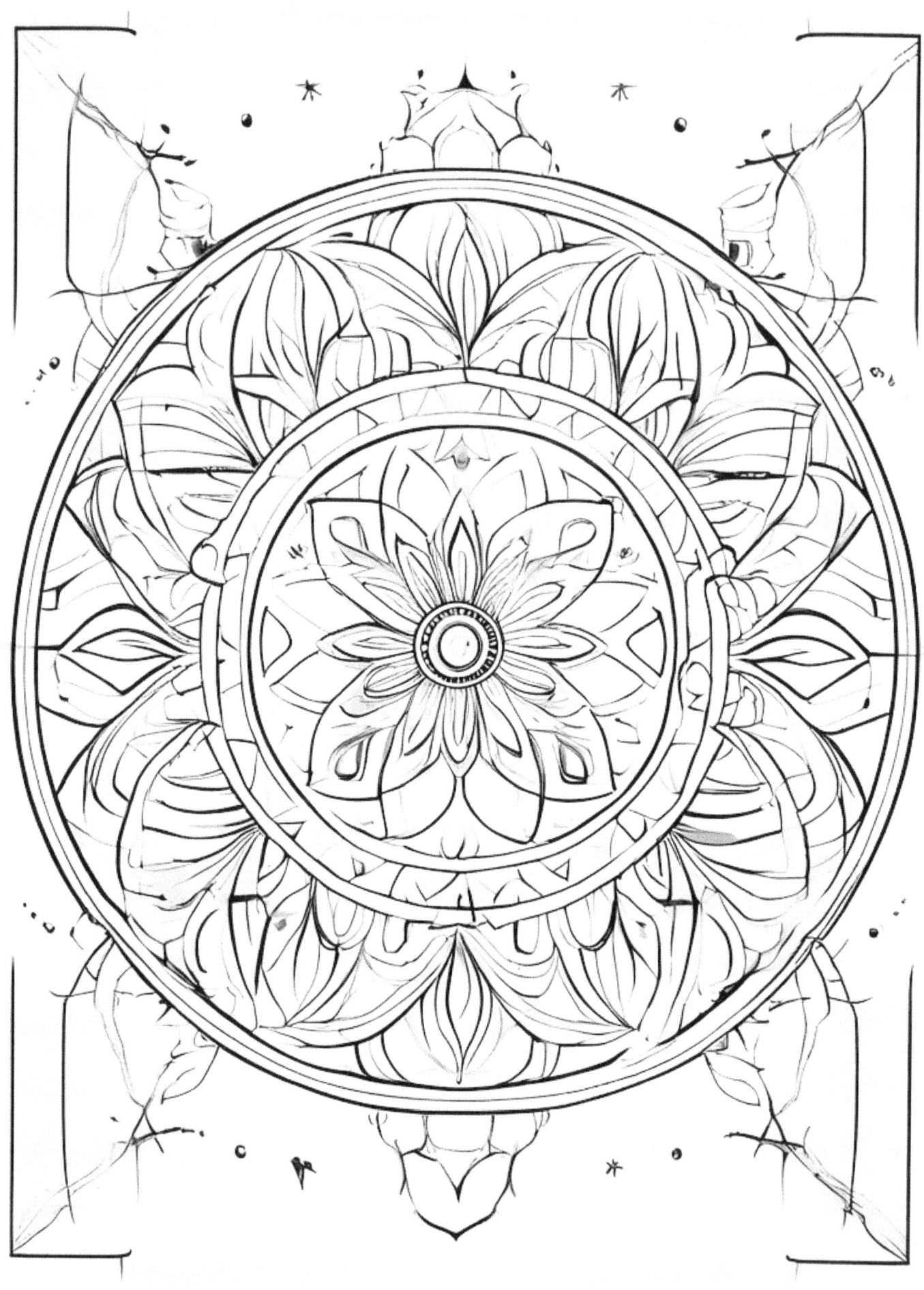

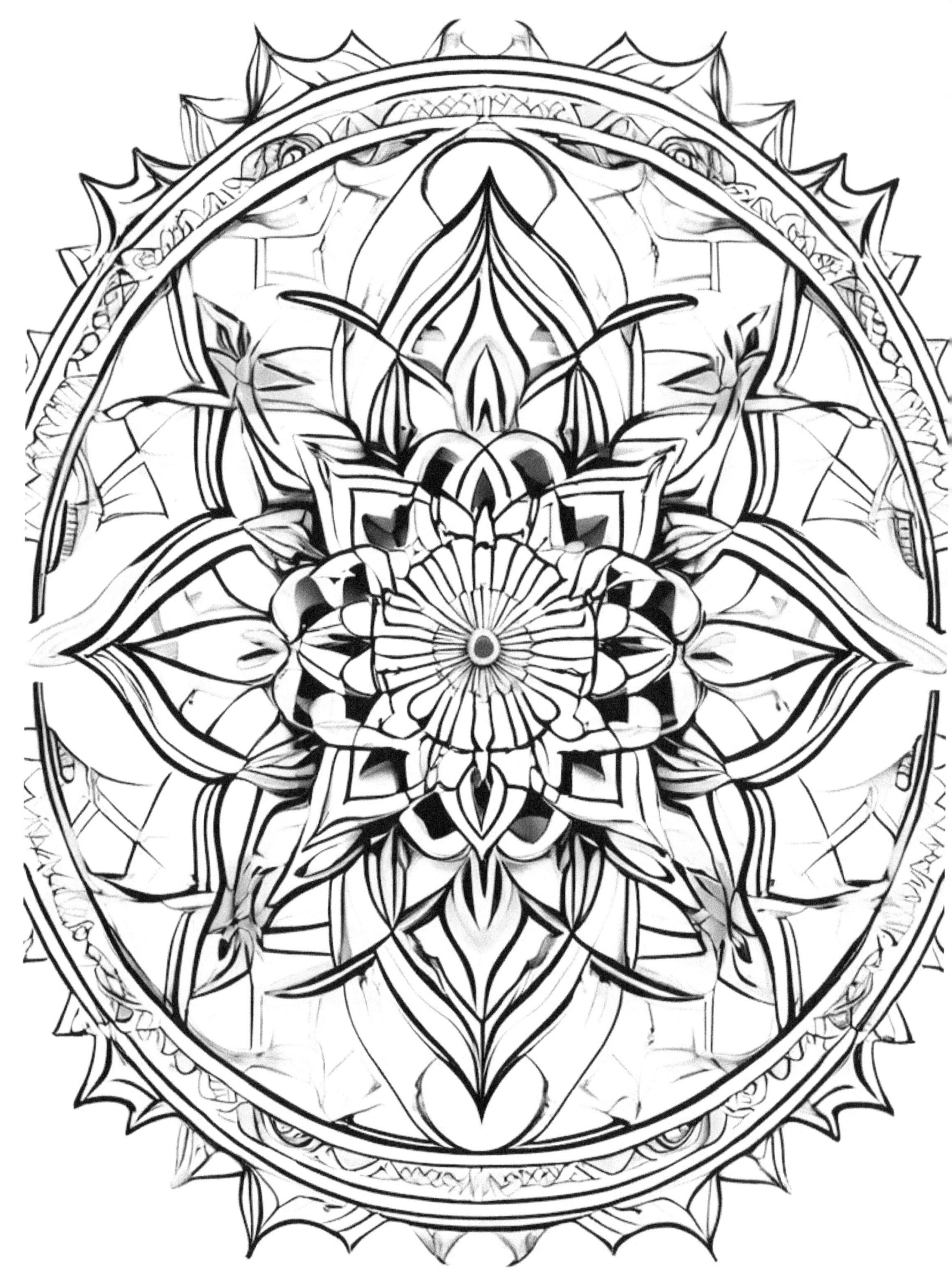

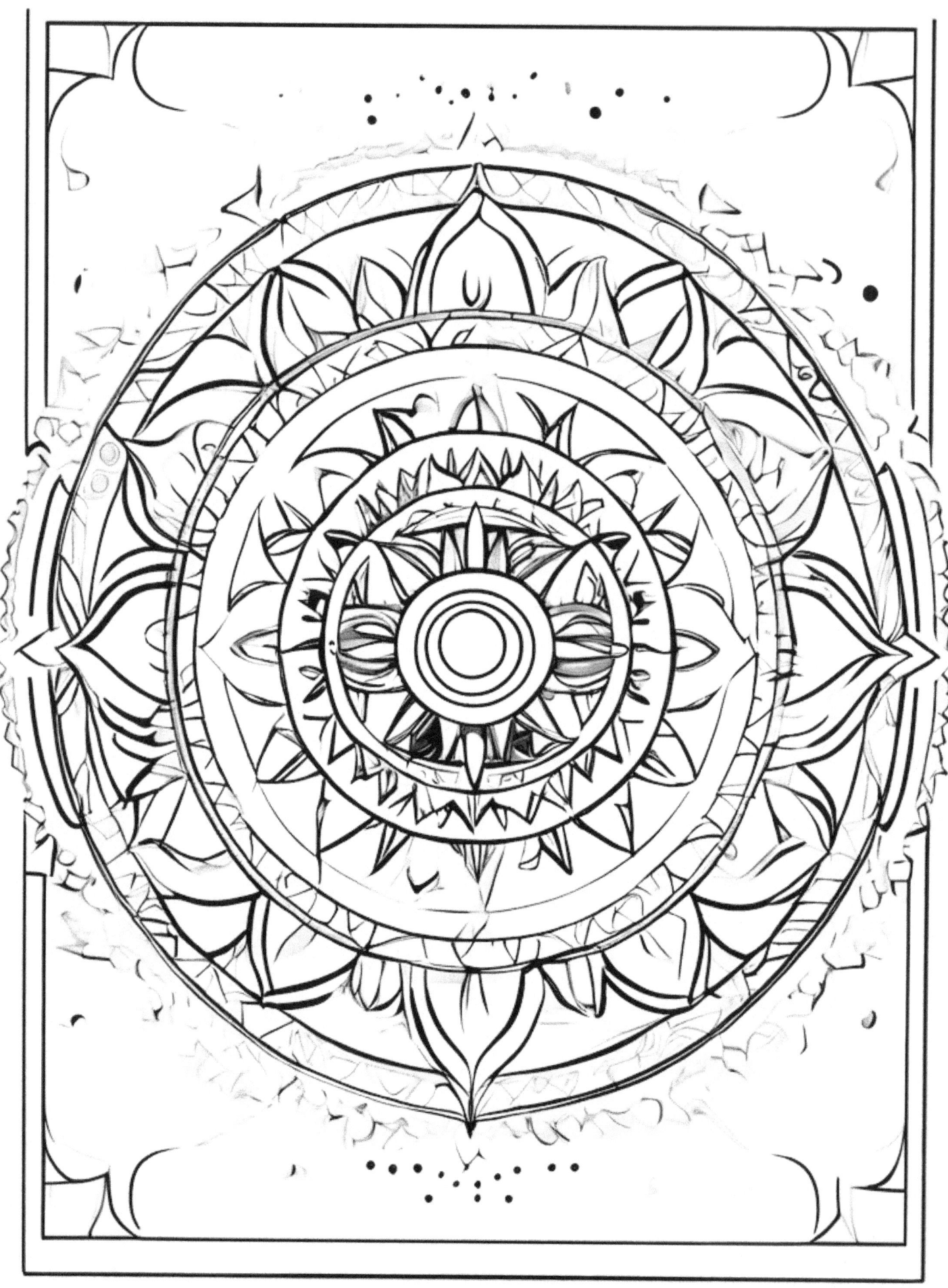

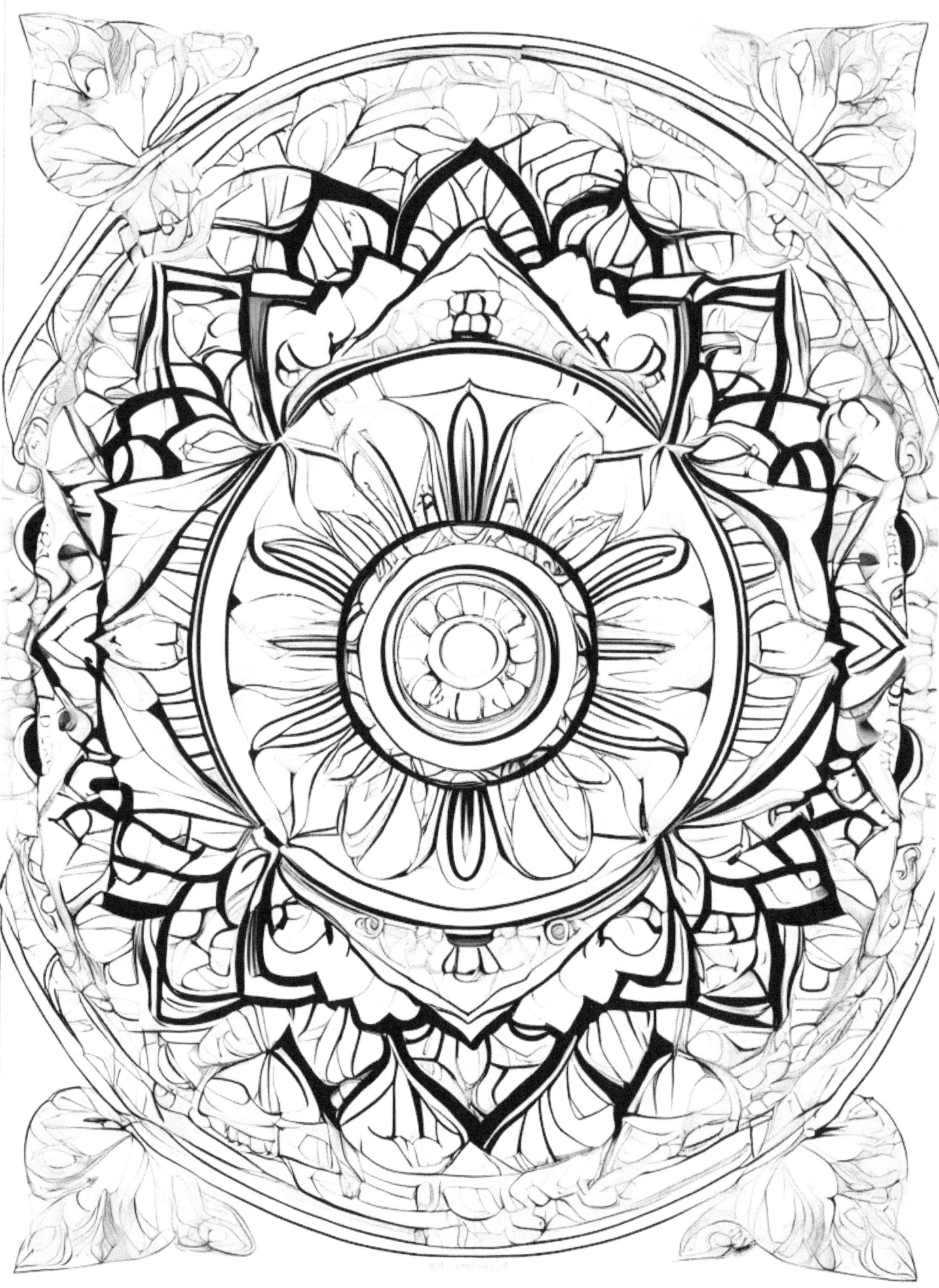

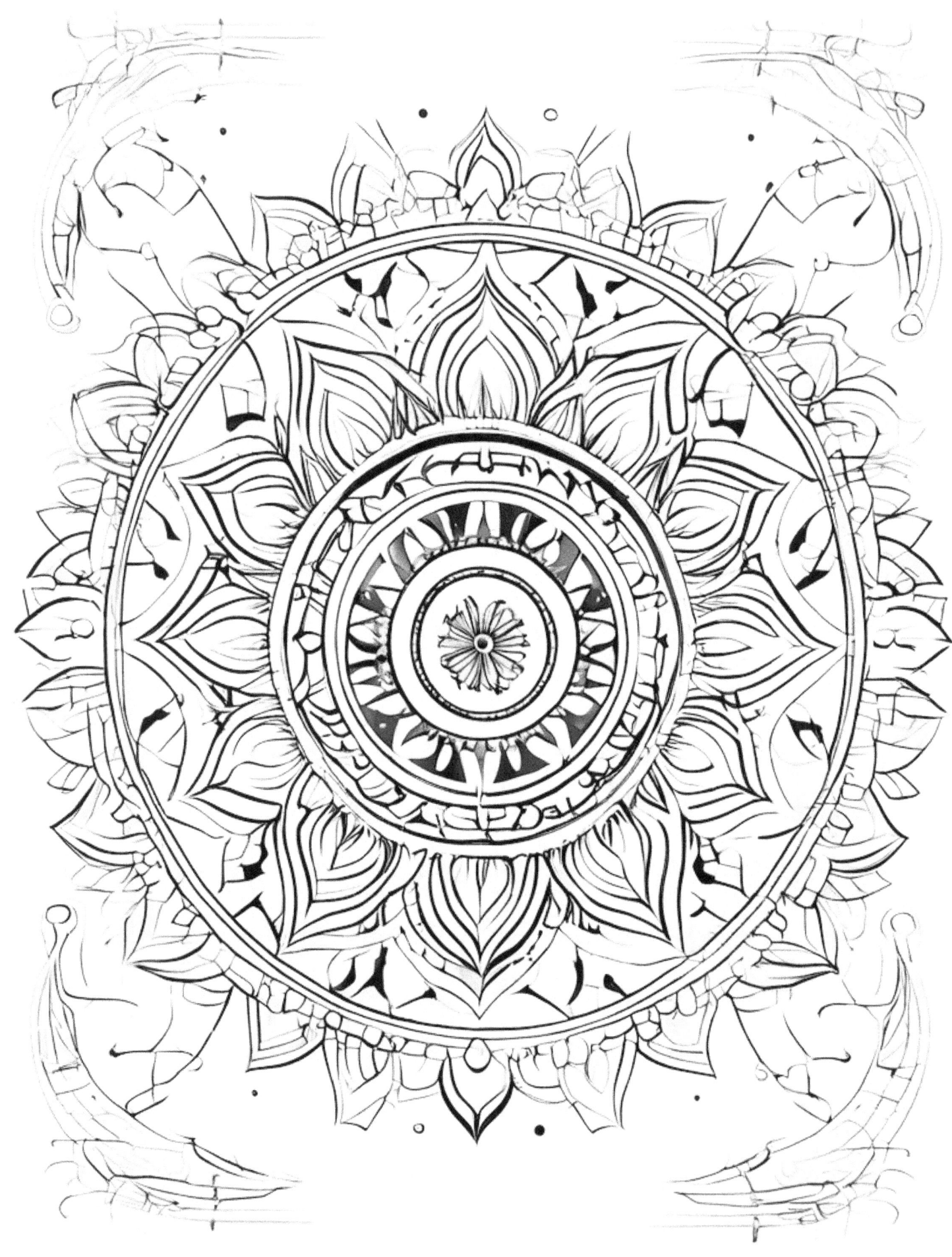

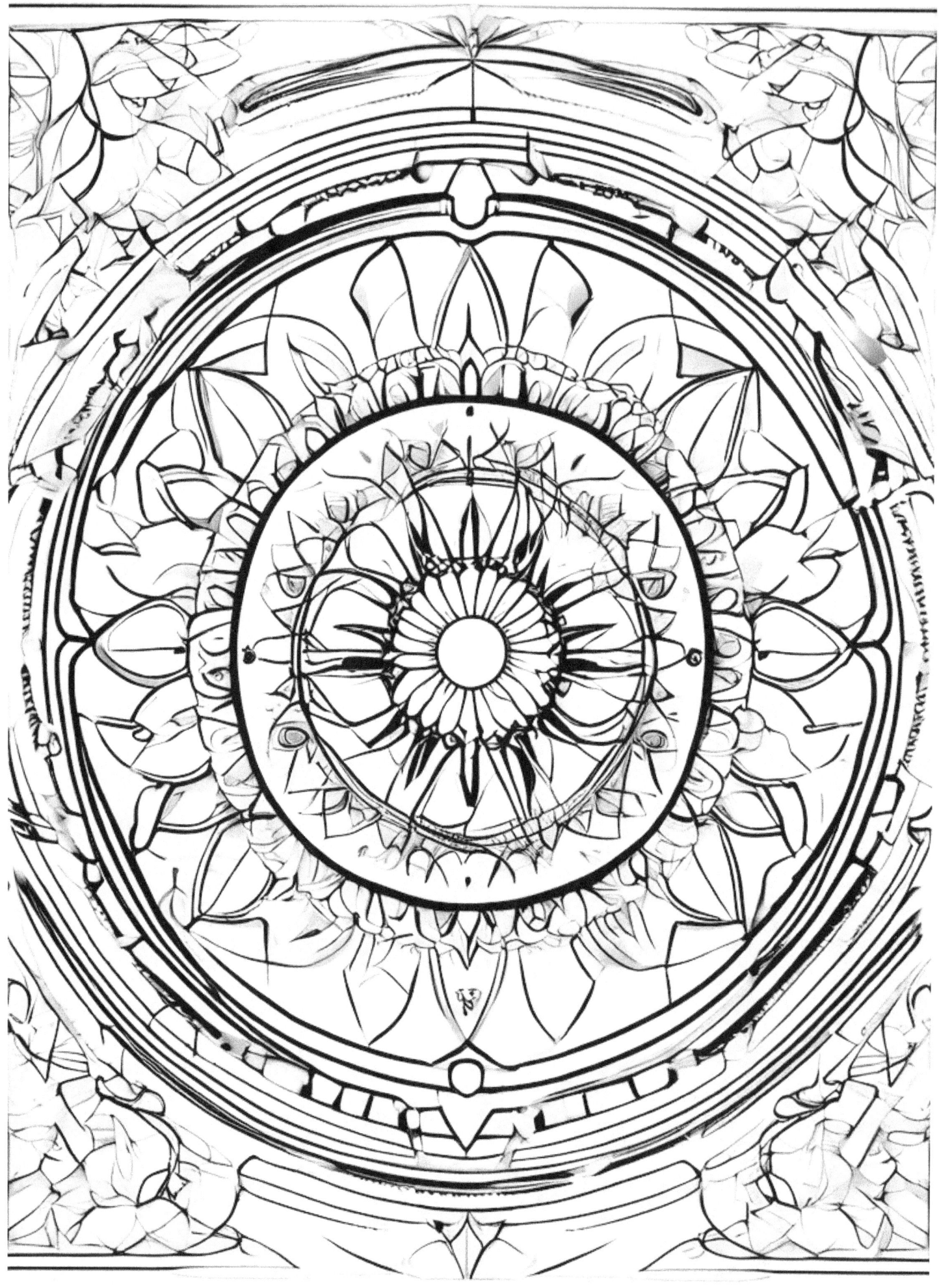

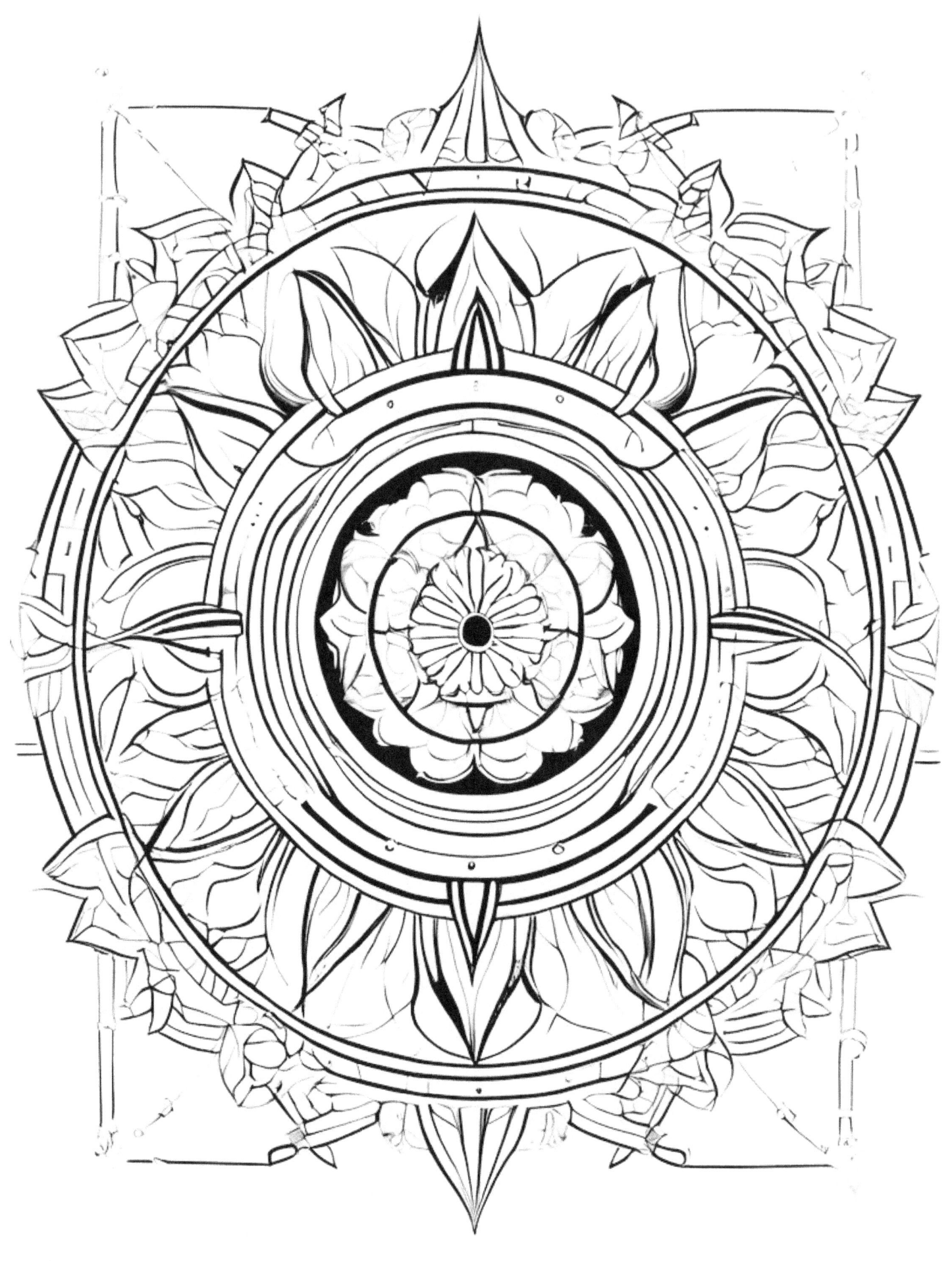

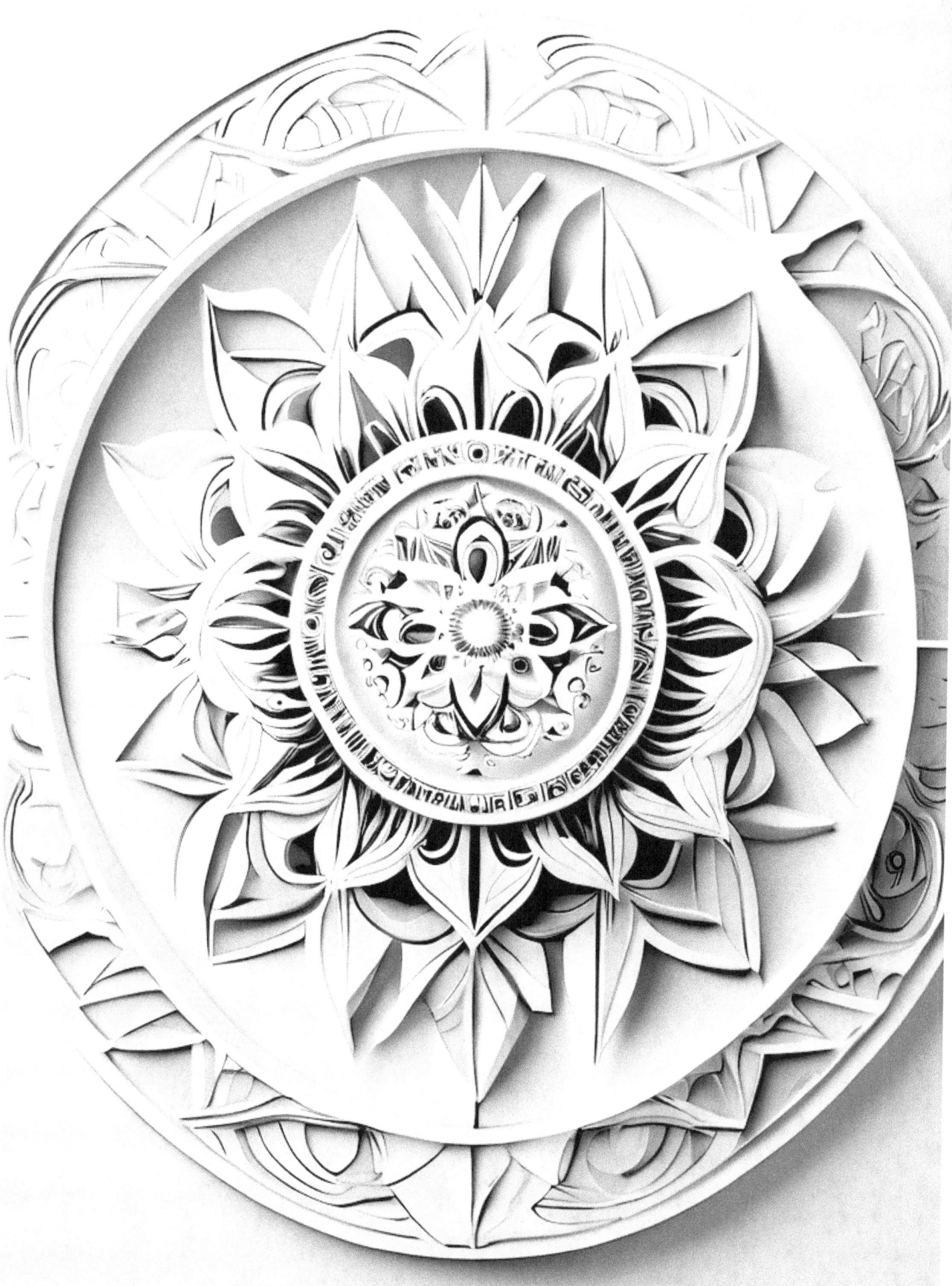

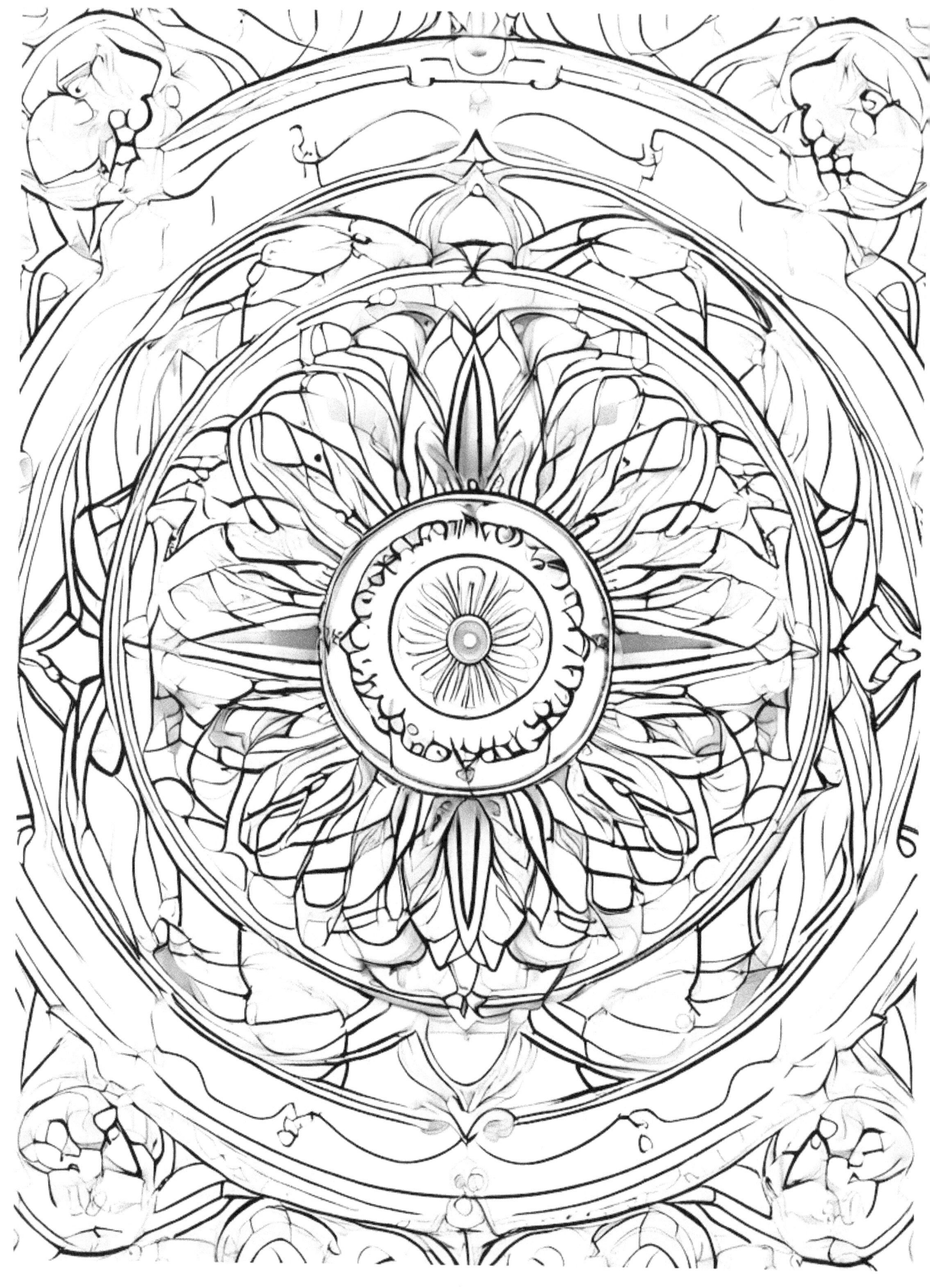

When you close this book, you complete not only a coloring journey, but also a journey of self-discovery and connection to the cosmos.

May the Celestial Mandalas you have found in these pages continue to inspire you even beyond this moment.

May they become vivid reminders of your journey of cosmic awakening, a constant reminder of the beauty and magic that permeates the cosmos.

May the stars continue to shine on your path, guiding you towards your own inner light.

May you always remember: you are made of stardust, shaped by the same matter that makes up stars and planets.

May this awareness guide you on your journey, reminding you of your eternal connection to the cosmos.

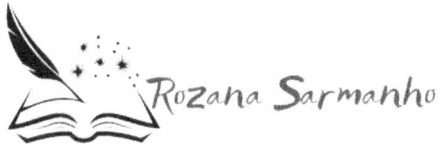